Observing Teacher Identities through Video Analysis

"What a valuable contribution this volume makes. It shows teacher educators how productive interactional awareness can be built and why it's worth the trouble. As the authors point out, discourse analysis is difficult and tedious work, yet key to teachers decomposing and improving their practice. By integrating theories and methods central to the creation of egalitarian, dialogic classrooms, without over-complicating or over-simplifying, the authors show us how to give teachers constructive tools for their pedagogical growth and regeneration."—Lesley A. Rex, University of Michigan, USA

"The authors offer compelling research that can help novice and practicing teachers explore their transactions with students and what these say about who they are as teachers and who they wish to be. This book provides the tools—theories of identity construction and video analysis techniques—to begin the deeply reflective process of how to be better teachers to all students and particularly those in non-dominant communities."—Althier Lazar, Saint Joseph's University, USA

"In their study of how preservice English teachers use identity as a lens to examine video recordings of their teaching, Vetter and Schieble provide a valuable approach for teacher educators to facilitate future teachers' awareness of classroom discourse."—Robert Petrone, Montana State University, USA

Teaching is often seen as an identity process, with teachers constructing and enacting their identities through daily interactions with students, parents, and colleagues. This volume explores how conducting video analysis helps teachers gain valuable perspectives on their own identities and improve classroom practice over time. This form of interactional awareness fosters reflection and action on creating classroom conditions that encourage equitable learning.

The volume follows preservice English teachers as they examine video records of their practice during student teaching, and how the evidence impacts their development as literacy teachers of diverse adolescents. By applying an analytic framework to video analysis, the authors demonstrate how novice teachers use positioning theory to transform their own identity performance in the classroom. Education scholars, teachers, and professional developers will greatly benefit from this unique perspective on teacher identity work.

Amy Vetter is Associate Professor of English Education at the University of North Carolina at Greensboro, USA.

Melissa Schieble is Assistant Professor of English Education at Hunter College of the City University of New York, USA.

Routledge Research in Teacher Education

The Routledge Research in Teacher Education series presents the latest research on Teacher Education and also provides a forum to discuss the latest practices and challenges in the field.
  Books in the series include:

Preparing Classroom Teachers to Succeed with Second Language Learners
  Lessons from a Faculty Learning Community
  Edited by Thomas H. Levine, Elizabeth R. Howard, and David M. Moss

Interculturalization and Teacher Education
  Theory to Practice
  Cheryl A. Hunter, Donna K. Pearson and A. Renee Gutiérrez

Community Fieldwork in Teacher Education
  Theory and Practice
  Heidi L. Hallman and Melanie N. Burdick

Portrait of a Moral Agent Teacher
  Teaching Morally and Teaching Morality
  Gillian R. Rosenberg

Observing Teacher Identities Through Video Analysis
  Practice and Implications
  Amy Vetter and Melissa Schieble

Observing Teacher Identities Through Video Analysis
Practice and Implications

Amy Vetter and Melissa Schieble

LONDON AND NEW YORK

First published 2016 by Routledge

2 Park Square, Milton Park, Abingdon, Oxon OX14 4RN
711 Third Avenue, New York, NY 10017, USA

Routledge is an imprint of the Taylor & Francis Group, an informa business

First issued in paperback 2017

Copyright © 2016 Taylor & Francis

The right of Amy Vetter and Melissa Schieble to be identified as author of this work has been asserted by them in accordance with sections 77 and 78 of the Copyright, Designs and Patents Act 1988.

All rights reserved. No part of this book may be reprinted or reproduced or utilised in any form or by any electronic, mechanical, or other means, now known or hereafter invented, including photocopying and recording, or in any information storage or retrieval system, without permission in writing from the publishers.

Notice:
Product or corporate names may be trademarks or registered trademarks, and are used only for identification and explanation without intent to infringe.

Library of Congress Cataloging-in-Publication Data
Vetter, Amy A., author.
　Observing teacher identities through video analysis : practice and implications / by Amy Vetter and Melissa Scheible.
　　　pages cm. — (Routledge research in teacher education)
　Includes bibliographical references and index.
　1. Observation (Educational method)　2. Teachers—Training of—Audio-visual aids.　3. Teachers—In-service training—Audio-visual aids.　4. Video tapes in education.　5. Teaching.　I. Scheible, Melissa, author.　II. Title.
　LB1731.6.V48 2016
　370.71'1—dc23　　　2015017307

ISBN: 978-1-138-83171-1 (hbk)
ISBN: 978-1-138-08594-7 (pbk)

Typeset in Sabon
by Apex CoVantage, LLC

This book is dedicated to all of the extraordinary educators who are mindful of their students' needs and who develop their practice based on those necessities.

We also dedicate this book to the support of our families. In particular, we are thankful for the two babies born while writing this book—Max and Della.

Contents

Acknowledgments ix

1 Introduction 1

2 Identity and Positionality: A Framework for Video Analysis of Teaching 10

3 Positions of Power 32

4 Positions of Advocacy 54

5 Positions of Facilitative Teaching 74

6 Positions of Critical and Racial Literacy 94

7 Implications for Identity Work and Video Analysis in Teacher Education 114

Appendix A: Video Analysis Assignment 127
Bibliography 129
Index 137

Acknowledgments

This book is the result of both formal and informal learning from colleagues and students interested in and/or resistant to becoming more aware of their practice. Because both Amy and Melissa come from an English background, the study of words is a challenging and inspiring practice. Thus, at the Literacy Research Association (LRA) conference in 2010, we discussed the idea of trying out a video assignment that asked preservice teachers to engage in discourse analysis of classroom interaction. Since then, we have been making sense of those analysis assignments and have grown significantly as teacher educators because of them.

With that said, we would like to thank our preservice teachers who allowed us to study their assignments and class discussions. We realize how vulnerable it can be to video record and analyze your first lessons. Because of your courage to delve into such rigorous work, we know that the readers of this book will learn more about how to become mindful of interactions and the ways in which they impact teacher and student identities. Because of your dedication, we have improved our own practice and learned more about what it means to foster the identity work of teacher candidates in a teacher education program.

We also want to acknowledge the mentorship of our candidates' cooperating teachers. Without their support and encouragement, our preservice teachers would not have the opportunity to try on various teacher identities before diving into their full-time career. Thank you for teaching them how to negotiate teacher identities in ways that best cultivate the reader and writer identities of the youth they teach. Along with acknowledgment of the cooperating teachers, we must say thanks for the patience and honesty of the students within those classrooms who allowed us to record their interactions. We cannot learn how to improve instruction without involving students.

Thanks to our colleagues over the past several years who reminded us to be mindful of our classroom interactions. In particular, thanks to Beth Maloch for introducing Amy to classroom discourse and discourse analysis during her studies at the University of Texas at Austin. Thanks to our colleagues at the Discourse Analysis Study Group at LRA (Melissa Wetzel, Julie Justice, and Christine Mallozzi) who helped us analyze several of these classroom interactions. Also, thanks to the Triad Teacher Researcher Group (Joy Myers and Holly Wroblewski), who also provided analytic insight into these classroom interactions and teacher reflections. Your multiple perspectives provided a more robust analysis of the study, which improved our practice and interpretations over time.

In addition, we would like to thank the people who conversed with us, read, and gave feedback throughout the process of writing this book. We especially thank Amy Johnson Lachuk for substantive feedback on our framework and Heidi Hallman for early support with the proposal process. We also thank Althier Lazar and colleagues for inviting us to present our work on video analysis and social equity teaching at LRA. This also includes our editors Stacy Noto, Christina Chronister, and Merritt Duncan. Thank you for your guidance.

Finally, we want to say thank you to our families who provided time and support for us to write this book. Jeff, Edie, and Della, Amy hopes to be mindful of her interactions with you in ways that foster, rather than hinder, your lifetime identity work. Melissa is grateful for the unwavering support and encouragement from her husband Chris during the writing of this book.

1 Introduction

We begin this book with a brief reflection on the usefulness of video analysis in learning to be a teacher from Harper,[1] one of our English teacher candidates:

> I think that despite the awkwardness of watching yourself teach, video analysis can be a valuable tool for teachers regardless of whether they're just starting out or whether they've been in the classroom for decades. Things look decidedly different from the front of the room sometimes, and it gives us an opportunity to see how our students see us rather than how we see our students and ourselves. You notice the weird little tics and habits you have. You notice your strengths and your flaws, and it allows you to think of ways that you can start thinking about modifying those behaviors that might be detrimental or distracting to your kids. It definitely helped me to think about my position as a teacher, both in how I presented myself to the kids and how the kids reacted to me. I enjoyed doing this because I think it taught me about how things look from the other side of the desk.

Harper's reflection about analyzing three video-recorded lessons during her student teaching experience highlights how videos can be used to see "how things look from the other side of the desk." The idea that teaching often looks different "from the front of the room" is a central focus of this book because it highlights the importance of examining pedagogy from multiple positionings. Thus, this book is for those of us interested in understanding and responding to students, colleagues, and everyday schooling events in ways that are consistent with our personal and professional ideas about teaching and learning as an adaptive process related to identity. We know that classroom demands and rewards are vast—our students have varying literacy needs, interests in popular culture, sports, or new media, and each bring their own social, cultural, and linguistic knowledge to the classroom. We balance the demands of our students' needs and interests with our own professional learning and personal lives—and at times struggle with the physical and emotional energy needed to improve and adapt to professional changes. We do all of this in a new era of accountability with new Common Core standards to align to our practices, new systems of teacher accountability, and what can feel like relentless pressures to prepare students for new state tests.

For beginning teachers, mitigating these multiple pressures makes the process of learning to teach a challenge. This book is about supporting new teachers with this very process—what we will refer to throughout as **teacher identity work**. Identity work, within the context of teacher education, is the opportunity for teachers to reflect on how they construct and enact teacher identities within moment-to-moment interactions and over time. Teacher identity work, then, is a productive challenge to align the multiple identities teachers desire to enact with what occurs in practice. Such identity work means being aware of how context shapes teacher identities and how teacher identities shape the world around them, including the agency to effect change. We view the process of learning to teach as inextricably tied to learning to enact teacher identities in a space where new teachers often struggle to be accepted members of an educational community. To foster teacher identity work, this book focuses on the analysis of classroom discourse, defined as naturally occurring talk and nonverbal communication (Cazden, 2001) that is captured by video. Thus, this book is about merging what we value as teachers, teacher educators, and education researchers to support new teachers to identify, analyze, and at times reimagine how what we know and do is enacted in the classroom. Although the research focus of the book is on preservice teacher education, we believe practicing teachers, administrators, literacy coaches, and teacher educators can also engage with identity work to improve their own practice or support novice or struggling teachers at their own schools.

As university-based teacher educators, we often asked ourselves the following question: How do teacher candidates engage in identity work and what can teacher educators do to support this process? To address that question, we present an assignment that integrates a discourse analytic framework with video analysis to aid novice teachers' identity work. In subsequent chapters, we illustrate the project through findings from a study of preservice English teachers who completed the video analysis assignment in two different English education programs in the southeast and northeast United States. To better understand what students learned from this analysis, we examine the following question: In what ways can discourse analysis of videotaped lessons foster the identity work of preservice teachers? In this opening chapter, we first situate our question within current research on the use of video as a tool for improving teacher and student learning.

TEACHER PREPARATION AND VIDEO ANALYSIS

To strengthen teacher preparation, researchers in education have looked within the field and to other professional schools (e.g., medicine) for guidance about the most effective ways to prepare novices to enter a professional field of practice (Grossman et al., 2009). Specifically, Grossman and her colleagues (2009) developed a framework to conceptualize constructs in teacher preparation that effectively scaffold and apprentice a novice teacher into teaching as a professional practice. We found their framework useful for locating how the tools we present in this book help novice teachers consider their identities as an integral part of the process of becoming a teacher. Grossman et al. examined practice-related courses (e.g., Methods courses) in teacher education and other professional fields such as the clergy to identify a set of practices that together encompass a framework for teacher preparation. Rather than defining practice as a discrete set of techniques or skills, they understand practice as that which "incorporates both intellectual and technical activities and that encompasses both the individual practitioner and the professional community" (p. 2059). To fully learn and continue a history of activities that define a particular community of practice (Lave & Wenger, 1991) community of practice, teacher must learn to engage in a complex negotiation of "understanding, skill, relationship, and identity" (Grossman et al., 2009, p. 2059). In this book, we focus on identity as an important part of learning to teach within these notions of practice.

Specifically, we find Grossman and her colleagues' (2009) constructs about representation, decomposition, and approximations of practice as a useful framework for thinking about how to help new teachers enter teaching as a professional practice. Representation comprises the various ways practice is made visible to candidates, including but not limited to in-person and video-based observations of classroom instruction. Decomposition considers how particulars of practice are broken down for the purpose of teaching and learning more about certain aspects or parts (e.g., vocabulary instruction or teacher and student relationships). The third part of their framework involves approximations of practice, or the opportunities novices have to engage in the practice with support (e.g., student teaching). We present research on a video analysis assignment that provides teacher candidates with specific tools for decomposing practice related to issues of language and identity. To support our decision to use video as a tool for helping novice teachers examine their identity work, we briefly turn to how and why video analysis has been leveraged in teacher education.

DECOMPOSING PRACTICE: VIDEO ANALYSIS OF TEACHING

We begin with a broad background on how video analysis has been used in teacher education, specifically as it relates to decomposing practice. We do so to situate our study within past and current efforts to understand the impact of this tool on novice teacher preparation and to frame areas where research is still needed. Over the past decade, much research has been published concerning why and how to address video analysis with novice teachers (Borko, Koellner, Jacobs, & Seago, 2011; Kleinknech & Schneider, 2013;

Tripp & Rich, 2012). What makes video such a valuable tool for novices? First, video-recorded classroom interactions allow teacher candidates to access practice in manageable segments (Le Fevre, 2004) and to view these segments from various vantage points (Spiro, Collins, & Ramchandran, 2007). Video cases have been used in teacher education to provide opportunities for teachers to take notice of interactions and events that were not easily observed while teaching (Sherin & van Es, 2009) and make connections between theory and practice (Brophy, 2004; Koc, Peker, & Osmoanoglu, 2009). Sherin and Russ (2015) note that, "because video provides a permanent record of classroom interactions, it can be viewed repeatedly and with different lenses in mind, promoting new ways for teachers to 'see' what is taking place" (p. 3). Teacher candidates who engage in this kind of analysis have been found to focus more on instruction during analysis than classroom management and write specific comments related to teaching and learning rather than on themselves (Rosaen, Lundeberg, Cooper, Fritzen, & Terpstra, 2008).

The digital aspect of recorded lessons can also provide opportunities for preservice teachers to slow down the fast pace of classroom events and concentrate on close analysis of specific moments (Sherin & Van Es, 2009; Van Es & Sherin, 2002). Sherin (2004) supports that video allows teacher candidates a window into teaching without the additional demands of being in the moment of complex classroom negotiations. Blomberg et al. (2013) further state that for novice teachers, "having to respond immediately to a teaching situation as is required during instruction can put a great deal of stress and pressure on novices and may interfere with their learning" (p. 93), whereas observing video lessens some of this pressure. Video also has been found to stimulate teacher candidates' interests in learning about practice (Lampert & Ball, 1998) and is considered a captivating tool (Roth, 2007). In addition, current policies support video analysis as a required skill of teachers in the future (Rich, 2015). Melissa can attest to the impact education policy in New York has had on requiring new teachers to video record and analyze their instruction as part of the edTPA (Education Teacher Performance Assessment). Such video analysis has opened opportunities for preservice teachers to engage in performance-based assessment that considers the cultural and linguistic backgrounds of students and expects candidates to articulate their practice. We do want to make it clear, however, that we do not promote standardized policies for teacher preparation. Video analysis has been shown to be useful for novice teachers due to the affordances of these tools and should be modified to fit multiple contexts.

Researchers also indicate that video analysis might lead to better teaching practices, which has the potential to improve student achievement (Labbo, Kinzer, Leu, & Teal, 2004). Much of the research in this area has been investigated in the context of math education. Borko, Jacobs, Eiteljorg and Pittman (2008) examined the use of video in math teacher learning communities and found that participants reported that watching video from their colleagues helped them learn new teaching techniques and better attend to students' thinking. Sherin and Han (2004) examined the use of video clubs as a model for professional development with middle school math teachers over the course of one year. They found that teachers' participation in video clubs resulted in more complex analysis of pedagogical issues and a greater focus on student thinking. Findings from these studies demonstrate that video analysis has the potential to help teachers also shift focus from their own performance (as has been the traditional emphasis with video reflections) to concentrate on how and why certain instructional methods result in improved student learning based on evidence from students' responses. Thus, video allows teachers to freeze moments in time and to problem solve complex classroom events from multiple viewpoints that include a shift toward student learning.

Additionally, a few studies have shown that video helps address the theory and practice conundrum in teacher education and supports teacher candidates to apply what they are learning at the university in the field, particularly in the areas of content knowledge, observational skills, and classroom management, when compared to using only written materials (Carlson & Falk, 1990; Overbaugh, 1995). Blomberg et al. (2013) note, however, that research on the effectiveness of using video in the context of preservice teacher education is still limited and that the ways that video is used in teacher preparation varies greatly. For future research, they suggest examining the details of how video analysis is utilized as an instructional tool in order to determine its effectiveness. To extend that need, van Es (2009) purports that video should be treated not as content, but as an instructional tool, and more work needs to understand how that tool works. Thus, in order to use video analysis effectively, teacher educators must develop "well-conceptualized learning environments" (Krammer et al., 2006, p. 94) that provide support for preservice teachers.

To build some guidance around the use of video in preservice teacher education, Blomberg and her colleagues discuss five research-based heuristics for creating learning environments that are conducive for teacher learning. These five heuristics include:

- A consideration of the learning goals that will be pursued
- Designing an activity that adheres to these goals that considers video as a tool to support pedagogical strategies (e.g., prompts or a specific focus or lens for viewing)
- Delineating carefully the video materials that support the learning goals (e.g., short clips from student teaching or a master teacher's videos)
- Addressing the strengths and limitations for video in preservice teacher education
- Aligning assessments to these instructional strategies and goals

The video analysis assignment presented in this book builds on each of these heuristics and demonstrates a well-conceptualized learning environment focused around issues of teacher identity. From the literature, few studies consider video analysis within the context of preservice teacher education (e.g., Santagata & Guarino, 2011), and none consider identity and positioning as an interpretive frame for video analysis. This book aims to address this gap and contextualize the use of video with an interpretive focus on identity. We draw on Sherin and Russ's (2015) notions of interpretive work with video as "meant to centralize and highlight the *active* sense making that teachers engage in as they observe classroom activity" (italics original, p. 8). Specifically, we became interested in how teachers used identity as a construct to actively make sense of what they noticed while viewing three videos from the student teaching experience. We came to this project knowing that novice teachers have desired identities they wish to enact in the classroom (e.g., teacher as facilitator), yet they have few tools to determine if the identities they desire to enact are achieved in the classroom. Building on identity and positioning as an interpretive lens for video analysis gave us the tools we needed to support this process. We discuss and model the specifics of this framework and the assignment in detail in Chapter Two. Below, we briefly describe the study to provide context for the book.

STUDY CONTEXT

We conducted a qualitative study in spring of 2012 to explore if and how the video analysis assignment helped preservice teachers examine how their teacher positionings within moment-to-moment interactions aligned or did not align with their desired identities during the student teaching experience. Overall findings from the study suggested that this assignment uncovered how all participants struggled to enact desired identities. Chapters Three through Six present cases that illustrate what teacher candidates learned from engaging in teacher identity work related to those struggles. Analysis within each of those cases includes both the perspective of the teacher candidate and teacher educators.

The study was conducted in two different English education programs in the northeast and southeast United States. Participants for the larger study were preservice English teachers (n=30) enrolled in a seminar course designed to support the student teaching experience. All participants were completing a university-based teacher preparation program toward initial certification in English (grades 7–12), of which the seminar and student teaching were the culminating experience. Amy and Melissa were the seminar instructors for each course at their respective institutions. After meeting at the Literacy Research Association Conference and discovering similar interests in teacher education and video analysis, Melissa and Amy worked together to develop this video assignment and study. They believed that gathering data from two different sites would provide more robust data and rich perspectives. Melissa's institution is a large, urban public university with a diverse student body of roughly 23,000 that includes a large population of immigrants and first generation college students. Many of her participants grew up in the city and surrounding areas where the college is located and demonstrate a commitment to return to teach in the city schools. Amy's university enrolls approximately 16,500 on-campus students each year. Most students who attend are White or African American and live in the surrounding area. Students join the School of Education from high school, community college, the military, and professional careers in education and beyond. The majority of teacher candidates are White, female, and middle-class who plan to teach within the area. They student teach in schools with students from diverse cultural and linguistic backgrounds.

For the assignment, student teachers videotaped their instruction three times at different points in the semester. For each of the three videos, candidates were required to transcribe or summarize 10–15 minutes of instruction and write a three-page reflection by engaging with the analytic tools. To study their interactions, candidates learned strategies to notice their language use and nonverbal communication as evidenced in the video and transcripts and to analyze what this meant about their identity work—ideas that will be fully explored in the next chapter. Through watching three videotaped lessons at different points in time over the semester, candidates reflected in writing on how what they noticed compared to and contrasted with their ideal teacher identities.

We prepared students for this assignment by discussing several articles related to how classroom interactions shape teacher and student identities. Specifically, those readings included excerpts from *Using Discourse Analysis to Improve Classroom Interaction* by Lesley Rex and Laura Schiller and *Choice Words* by Peter Johnston. As a whole group, we watched a videotaped classroom interaction from *The Teaching Channel* and examined the assignment questions. We then discussed the advantages and disadvantages of this analysis. Topics included uncovering misalignments, the tediousness of this kind of examination, and the influence of students' personal identities and schooling history on the enactment of their own teaching identities.

This book is organized to present findings from our research and offer practical suggestions for applying this work to other contexts. In the next chapter, we describe and explain how theories about identity and positioning informed the analytic framework designed for the video analysis assignment. We also discuss the assignment in detail, including how methods associated with discourse analysis were invoked to help preservice teachers analyze their videos. The second half of Chapter Two is devoted to an example of how one teacher candidate named Hannah completed the assignment to examine her desired identities in practice. Hannah's example is meant to help readers apply aspects of the framework discussed in the chapter to an actual transcript. In addition, this example provides a snapshot for the more in depth analyses presented by each case in Chapters Three through Six.

Each of the case studies presented in Chapters Three through Six focuses on a different desired identity enactment that was salient for our teacher candidates. You will read about Jay, who struggled with enacting a critical pedagogy teacher identity and managing positions of power in the classroom. Then, we will explore Erica, who desired to be a caring advocate for her students during her student teaching experience in a "second chance" school for students who have struggled emotionally and academically. Jaina, in Chapter Five, desired to be a facilitator, yet struggled to use language to enact this identity and position herself and her students in ways that invited classroom dialogue. In Chapter Six, you will read about how students engaged in critical conversations about how specific identity markers (e.g., race, class, gender, and sexual orientation) shaped teacher positionings. To further highlight the framework in each subsequent chapter, we include excerpts from classroom transcripts to provide opportunities for readers to engage in specific elements of analysis. Finally, the book will conclude with implications for identity work and video analysis in teacher education.

NOTE

1. Pseudonyms are used throughout this text.

REFERENCES

Blomberg, G., Renkl, A., Sherin, M. G., Borko, H., & Seidel, T. (2013). Five research-based heuristics for using video in preservice teacher education. *Journal for Educational Research Online, 5*(1), 3–33.

Borko, H., Jacobs, J., Eiteljorg, E., & Pittman, M. E. (2008). Video as a tool for fostering productive discussions in mathematics professional development. *Teaching and Teacher Education, 24*, 417–436.

Borko, H., Koellner, K., Jacobs, J., & Seago, N. (2011). Using video representations of teaching in practice-based professional development programs. *ZDM, 43*(1), 175–187.

Brophy, J. (2004). Discussion. In J. Brophy (Ed.), *Using video in teacher education: Advances in research on teaching* (Vol. 10, pp. 287–304). Amsterdam: Elsevier.

Carlson, H. L., & Falk, D. R. (1990). Effectiveness of interactive videodisc instructional programs in elementary teacher education. *Journal of Educational Technology Systems, 19*(2), 151–163.

Cazden, C. (2001). *Classroom discourse: The language of teaching and learning.* Portsmouth, NH: Heinemann.

Grossman, P., Compton, C., Igra, D., Ronfeldt, M., Shahan, E., & Williamson, P. W. (2009). Teaching practice: A cross-professional perspective. *Teachers College Record, 111*(9), 2055–2100.

Kleinknecht, M., & Schneider, J. (2013). What do teachers think and feel when analyzing videos of themselves and other teachers teaching? *Teaching and Teacher Education, 33*, 13–23.

Koc, Y., Peker, D., & Osmoanoglu, A. (2009). Supporting teacher professional development through online video case study discussions: An assemblage of preservice and inservice teachers and the case teacher. *Teaching and Teacher Education, 8*, 1158–1168.

Krammer, K., Ratzka, N., Klieme, E., Lipowsky, F., Pauli, C., & Reusser, K. (2006). Learning with classroom videos: Conception and first results of an online teacher-training program. *Zeitschrift für Didaktik der Mathematik, 38*(5), 422–432.

Labbo, L. D., Kinzer, C. K., Leu, D., & Teal, W. H. (2004). Technology: Connections that enhance children's literacy acquisition and reading achievement. In *Case Technologies to Enhance Literacy Learning*. Retrieved October 26, 2013, from http://ctell.uconn.edu/cases.htm

Lampert, M., & Ball, D. L. (1998). *Teaching, multimedia, and mathematics: Investigations of real practice*. New York, NY: Teachers College Press.

Lave, J., & Wenger, E. (1991). *Situated learning: Legitimate peripheral participation*. Cambridge, UK: Cambridge University Press.

Le Fevre, D. M. (2004). Designing for teacher learning: Video-based curriculum design. In J. Brophy (Ed.), *Using video in teacher education* (pp. 235–258). Amsterdam, Netherlands: Elsevier.

Overbaugh, R. C. (1995). The efficacy of interactive video for teaching basic classroom management skills to pre-service teachers. *Computers in Human Behavior, 11*(3–4), 511–527.

Rich, P. (2015). Examining the role of others in video self analysis. In B. Calandra & P. J. Rich (Eds.), *Digital video for teacher education: Research and practice* (pp. 71–88). New York: Routledge.

Rosaen, C., Lundeberg, M., Cooper, M., Fritzen, A., & Terpstra, M. (2008). Noticing noticing: How does investigation of video records change how teachers reflect on their experiences? *Journal of Teacher Education, 59*(4), 347–360.

Roth, W. M. (2007). Epistemic mediation: Video data as filters for the objectification of teaching by teachers. In R. Goldman, R. Pea, B. Barron, & S. J. Derry (Eds.), *Video research in the learning sciences* (pp. 367–382). Mahwah, NJ: Lawrence Erlbaum.

Santagata, R., & Guarino, J. (2011). Using video to teach future teachers to learn from teaching. *ZDM the International Journal of Mathematics Education, 43*(1), 133–145.

Sherin, M. G. (2004). New perspectives on the role of video in teacher education. In J. Brophy (Ed.), *Using video in teacher education* (pp. 1–27). New York: Elsevier Science.

Sherin, M. G., & Han, S. (2004). Teacher learning in the context of a video club. *Teaching and Teacher Education, 20*, 163–183.

Sherin, M. G., & Russ, R. S. (2015). Teacher noticing via video: The role of interpretive frames. In B. Calandra & P.J. Rich (Eds.), *Digital video for teacher education: Research and practice* (pp. 3–20). New York: Routledge.

Sherin, M. G., & van Es, E. (2009). Effects of video club participation on teacher's professional vision. *Journal of Teacher Education, 60*(1), 20–37.

Spiro, R. J., Collins, B. P., & Ramchandran, A. (2007). Reflections on a post-Gutenberg epistemology of video use in ill-structured domains: Fostering complex learning and cognitive flexibility. In R. Goldman, R. Pea, B. Barron, & S. J. Derry (Eds.), *Video research in the learning sciences* (pp. 93–100). Mahwah, NJ: Lawrence Erlbaum.

Tripp, T., & Rich, P. (2012). Using video to analyze one's own teaching. *British Journal of Educational Technology, 43*(4), 678–704.

van Es, E. (2009). Participants' roles in the context of a video club. *Journal of the Learning Sciences, 18*(1), 100–137.

van Es, E., & Sherin, M. G. (2002). Learning to notice: Scaffolding new teachers' interpretations of classroom interactions. *Journal of Technology and Teacher Education, 10*(4), 571–596.

2 Identity and Positionality
A Framework for Video Analysis of Teaching

We open this chapter with a story from Hannah, who is a teacher candidate in a high school English classroom. Hannah (a young, White, middle-class female) completed her student teaching at Smartsville High School, a rural school in the southeast United States. The majority of students in her classroom were White, with a small number of African American and Latino/as students all coming from lower and middle-class backgrounds. In the reflection below, Hannah described a video-recorded and transcribed lesson from a tenth-grade honors English classroom in which she facilitated discussion about heroic traits. This discussion was meant to provoke interest in and build prior knowledge about Hercules. In her writing, she reflected on the ways in which her talk shaped how she positioned herself as a teacher and how her students situated her as a teacher.

> As far as the discussion is concerned, I try to position myself as a facilitator or "conversation jockey," posing questions to the students and allowing them to "bounce" answers off one another—sometimes students will ask questions to one another (as occurred in the video at least once) as a result of the conversation. I prefer to facilitate/elaborate on statements rather than dominate the conversation. My students appeared to position me as a relaxed authority figure—I can be joked around with, we can have little tangents on occasion, we can laugh as a class—but I think they are also well aware of my expectations. I think they also position me as someone who gives them approval. This is an Honors level course and it seems as though discussions can almost become a quest for my affirmation that they've done the right thing and this continues to be my main issue with class discussions. . . . Also, as the discussion progresses, there were about ten names/voices I kept hearing over and over again. I think that volunteering is great, but there are twenty other students in the room who aren't speaking up/raising their hands as much as those ten, and I really need to work on incorporating them into the discussion more. . . . I don't want to set a limit to student comments or anything like that . . . but I need to figure out how to achieve a balance as far as everyone having something to

say. . . . Perhaps simply calling on quiet students and asking what they thought might help.

In the above assigned reflection, Hannah recognized that she successfully positioned herself as a facilitator by posing questions and allowing students to share ideas with one another. This recognition of her interactions connected with Hannah's teacher philosophy statement that described her ideal classroom as one that is open and interactive. We asked students to write or revise a teacher philosophy statement at the beginning of English methods and post it online for students, parents, and colleagues to see. By teacher philosophy, we mean a statement that provides a clear, concise description of their teaching approach, methods, and expertise. Although she seemed pleased with her enactments, she mentioned that she is not comfortable when students positioned her as teacher who gives approval and affirmation for what is "right" during discussion because it does not foster an open and interactive classroom. She also expressed concern with calling on the same students during a whole group discussion, which potentially only positioned a small portion of her students as participants. As a result, she proposed the possible solution of finding strategies for increasing participation among the quiet students by encouraging them to express their thoughts.

As teacher educators, we value opportunities in the classroom when teacher candidates openly discuss the construction and enactment of their teacher identities. For Hannah, this meant analyzing a moment in which she noticed the complexity of her desired facilitator position. Specifically, in her reflection, she pinpointed specific kinds of talk (e.g., posing questions) that positioned her as a facilitator and interactional patterns (e.g., calling on the same students) that did not foster that facilitator position. With this interactional awareness, Hannah was able to develop concrete ways in which she could foster contributions from more of her students (e.g., calling on quiet students) in the future.

We share the above example to illustrate our belief that awareness of the construction and enactment of particular teacher identities (e.g., Hannah as facilitator) is an important part of the learning process for preservice teachers. Significant moment-to-moment interactions with students during instructional time can be fleeting and largely unrealized by novice and experienced teachers alike; yet, these moments may (and often do) build over time to construct particular identities that have a profound impact on both the individual and the students for whom teachers care. Those who have taken on the role of supporting new or struggling teachers know that moving out of survival mode toward in-the-moment awareness of one's practice is slow, deliberate, and at times painstaking work. In this chapter, we present a framework, grounded in research about teacher identity (Alsup, 2006), which can be applied to video analysis to support teachers in building the kind of interactional awareness that Hannah demonstrated.

THEORIES ABOUT IDENTITY

To further conceptualize theories of identity in relation to learning and teaching, we provide a brief history of identity theories and describe three interrelated characteristics that we use throughout this book. The term identity has a long history that must be explored in order to understand how it is used today in relation to teacher education. Early theories of identity used the term to describe a stable and achieved self (Erickson, 1968). Such theories evolved as social psychologists noted the dynamic processes of identity construction that occur through social interactions (Mead, 1934; Vygotsky, 1978). Later, sociologists and anthropologists (e.g., Bourdieu, 1991) redefined the term to include cultural identity to recognize how individuals are shaped through cultural markers and social positionings. Most contemporary educational scholars, then, draw from multiple fields (e.g., anthropology, psychology, poststructuralism, sociology, and sociolinguistics) to define concepts of identity within education (Bourdieu, 1986; Butler, 1993; Gee, 2000; Holland, Skinner, Lachicotte, & Cain, 1998; Lave & Wenger, 1991).

For this book, we draw from a theoretical framework that views identity as a process in which people learn how to talk and behave in ways that gain them status and membership in a social group (Brtizman, 1991; Gee, 2005; Holland et al., 1998; Lave & Wenger, 1991). Specifically, we use Holland et al.'s (1998) definition of identities as "self-understandings" or a "key means through which people care about and care for what is going on around them" (Holland et al., 1998, p. 5). Because identities are constantly evolving and are shaped by social, cultural, and political contexts, we discuss identities as fluid, dynamic, and discursively constructed (Holland, et al., 1998; Mishler, 2004). For this book, we build from the following four interrelated characteristics of these theories that we discuss below: 1) identities are fluid; 2) identities are shaped through discursive interactions; 3) identities are shaped by social, political, and cultural contexts; 4) individual's identities also shape the world around them.

Theorists argue that identities are fluid, multiple, and dynamic (Mishler, 2004) and are constructed, enacted, or narrated over time (Anzaldua, 1999; Sfard & Prusak, 2005). Thus, a teacher is not a fixed way of being. Instead, teachers take on various identities (e.g., coach) over time that shift depending on students, colleagues, and experiences. Although identity enactments vary depending on various contexts, people also retain histories of participation that shape how they accept or resist identities within those contexts (Holland et al., 1998). For instance, a teacher might recognize that past instructors impact how they currently teach in their classroom. Teacher identities, then, are constructed through an ongoing process of interpretation and reinterpretation of experiences (Kerby, 1991), a notion that corresponds with the idea that "becoming" a teacher is a process of lifelong learning (e.g., Beijaard, Meijer, & Verloop, 2004; Day, 1999).

In relation to the recognition that identities are dynamic, we also understand that identities are shaped by and performed through discursive interactions (Holland et al., 1998). When people communicate with one another, they generally have awareness of the social groups with which they wish to identify and adjust their language and behaviors accordingly. Gee (2005) refers to this as having an "identity kit" or performing ways of being in the world that include speech, gestures, dress, and other nonverbal behaviors. For educators, this means that teacher identities are positions that are accepted and/or resisted through interactions with students, parents, and colleagues. For example, a colleague might position a fellow teacher as an expert in math literacy during a discussion in a professional learning community. That teacher might take up that position by sharing ideas about how to integrate math journals into lessons that challenge students to problem-solve. That teacher, then, enacts teacher identities related to her expertise in math literacy. Paying attention to such discursive moments can provide insight into the identities that we construct and enact over time.

We also understand that identities are shaped by social, political, and cultural contexts. Enacting a particular identity in a particular situation enables individuals to acquire social status, such as making new friends or receiving a raise. For instance, knowing how to use academic language to construct an argumentative essay in college brings one the social good of a positive grade and the identity of a "good student," which often opens doors for acquiring other areas of social status, such as a higher salary. Thus, students who have had unequal access to knowledge and skills necessary to perform a "good student" identity may be recognized by others as a "struggling learner" and, as a result, do not earn the social status needed to flourish in the context of school. Therefore, the identities one enacts are always tailored to the purpose of belonging to a particular social group (e.g., "good students") that has established (and often institutionally bound) norms for participation over time. Teacher identities, then, are shaped by past experiences, such as education or family and community experiences (Cooper & Olsen, 1996; Sugrue, 1997). That prior knowledge or set of internal narratives defines their understanding of teachers and how (or what knowledge) children learn, which can be difficult to broaden in scope (Alsup, 2006). This is related to the concept that specific identities are enacted in order for the individual to be recognized and gain membership into that community. Learning to be a teacher then involves knowledge of a school community's social and cultural beliefs and practices (Weber, 1991). For preservice teachers, this means that in order to be recognized as a teacher by colleagues, parents, students, and university supervisors, they must use language and behaviors (e.g., collaborate with others, attend meetings) that others within that context associate with "being" a teacher. As a result, teacher candidates will be shaped by what that context values, such as performance data or teacher leadership. How one learns to be recognizable as a teacher in a school is highly subject to institutional norms and current social and political debates on what constitutes effective teaching and learning. In the teacher education programs where we (two English Education professors) teach, effective teaching is demonstrated by developing a

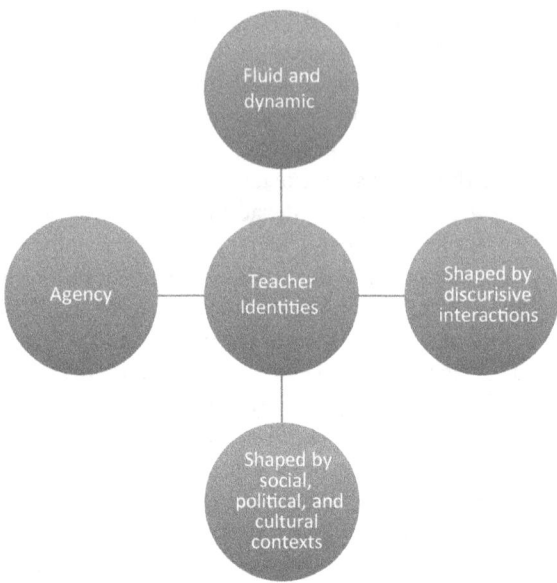

Figure 2.1 Teacher Identities

supportive learning environment that builds on diverse students' cultural, social, and linguistic needs and interests as a foundation for literacy learning (Gay, 2010). Thus, preservice teachers are encouraged to adopt a culturally responsive teacher identity.

Teachers, however, are not powerless. Oftentimes, educators act as agents who shape the world around them (i.e., school or classroom) (Florio-Ruane, 2002). Individuals, in this case teachers, use resources around them in order to "craft a response in a time and space defined by others' standpoints in activity, that is, in a social field conceived as the ground of responsiveness. Human agency comes through this art of improvisation" (Holland et al., 1998, p. 272). Practically, this means that teachers can change curriculum and policies within their departments and schools in ways that align with their beliefs about pedagogy. For instance, a teacher might change how writing is taught at her school by researching and implementing writing workshop methods in a school that traditionally valued skill and drill writing instruction (Vetter, Myers, & Hester 2014). Agency, then, can be a way for individuals to redefine accepted identities within specific contexts.

IDENTITY WORK IN TEACHER EDUCATION

Scholars (Alsup, 2006; Beijaard et al., 2004) have used theories of identity to frame educational research in several areas. To learn more about how that lens has helped educators make sense of teaching and learning, we discuss those areas of scholarship below. We follow that discussion with an examination of what has not yet been explored and how our research fills that gap.

Teacher education research has used an identity framework to examine how identity markers (e.g., race or gender) shape teacher identities (DeCorse & Vogtle, 1997). For example, scholars have investigated issues of race and power in education by exploring how the racial attitudes voiced by White teachers shape pedagogy and classroom interactions (Pennington, 2007; Vaught & Castagno, 2008). For example, Pennington (2007) explored how preservice teachers' White identities impacted how they viewed children of color in their classrooms. Through seminar conversations about their teaching experiences, she found common threads that included the language of saving and/or rescuing children of color from lives that the teachers perceived to be missing essential qualities. Pennington found that through personal stories related to her own teaching, she and her students were able to review and renew their narratives as White teachers and be honest about how their race impacted their views of students. They learned that it was okay to talk about race and discuss the complexities of how it shaped their daily interactions and assumptions about students' learning experiences. This work, then, recognizes how identity markers are related to issues of power that impact students' learning experiences (Freedman & Appleman, 2008). For some student teachers, this means examining the specific ways in which identity markers impact learning and instruction so that they can negotiate positions of power with students in ways that foster learning opportunities (Vetter, Meacham, & Schieble, 2013).

Scholarship on teacher identities also examines how preservice teachers negotiate the conflicting discourses of their university and school (Brtizman, 1991; Cooper and Olson, 1996; Sexton, 2008) and how those negotiations shape teacher identities (Alsup, 2006; Danielwitz, 2001; Ronfeldt & Grossman, 2008). Preservice teachers involved in student teaching experiences must enact identities consistent with school norms in ways that afford them teacher status and membership (Coldron & Smith, 1999; Haniford, 2010). They must also learn to negotiate multiple ideologies from personal, professional, and institutional contexts in order to perform teacher identities that align with their teacher beliefs (Alsup, 2006). For instance, a student teacher might believe in a collaborative learning approach. This might conflict, however, with a cooperating teacher who focuses on direct instruction. As a result, the student teacher will need to figure out ways to merge collaborative learning with direct instruction as a way to situate herself as the kind of teacher she envisions while also respecting the wishes of her cooperating teacher. For student teachers, then, constructing teacher identities consists of borrowing, negotiating, and claiming ownership in a space that is not their own (Britzman, 1994). As a result, many student teachers think it is best to perform the esteemed identities of their cooperating teachers, facilitators, professors, and even students to prosper. For those that resist those valued identities, they run the risk of being ostracized from the school community. If that happens, teachers leave the profession or they conform to their school's belief systems despite conflicting beliefs. These tensions can also negatively impact instruction and learning in the classroom, and potentially the quality of instruction and school-wide achievement (Rex & Schiller, 2009). Thus, in order to be fruitful at these negotiations, teachers must merge individual beliefs of what it means to be a teacher with professional identities (i.e., borderland discourses) (Alsup, 2006).

To help with those complex mediations, research has also focused on the role of teacher education in supporting teachers to notice and use theories about identity to grow as practitioners (Horn, Nolen, Ward, & Campbell, 2008; Ma & Singer-Gabela, 2011). Overall, focusing on identity work in courses has been found to help teacher candidates enact agency within their school (Fairbanks et al., 2010), modify assumptions about what it means to be teacher (Horn et al., 2008) and opens new possibilities for ways of "being" a teacher (Ma & Singer-Gabella, 2011). Program components, such as ongoing communication, support, opportunities to reflect, occasions to practice, and constructive feedback from multiple points of view have been found to be helpful ways to foster the identity work of teachers (Freedman & Appleman, 2008). Specifically, research found that preservice teachers working in urban schools benefitted from being in a cohort over several years because it provided a space for teachers with different backgrounds and experiences to support each other, even after graduation (Freedman & Appleman, 2008). Specifically, these cohorts fostered opportunities for conversation that included reflection and feedback about instructional practices they were practicing in their classrooms (Freedman & Appleman, 2008). Cohorts, however, can also intensify problems, particularly when conversations are not constructive. Implications from such studies suggest that teacher education programs are ideal spaces for preservice teachers to try on possible teacher identities in a supportive context (Ronfeldt & Grossman, 2008).

Educators, however, would benefit from more research that examines how novice teachers enact, notice, analyze, and at times adjust their classroom identity work in their teacher education courses. We argue that discourse analysis of classroom interactions captured through video is one way for teacher candidates to critically examine how they construct and enact teacher identities over time. Scholarship illustrates the important relationship between discursive interactions and learning (Allington, 2002; Applebee, Langer, Nystrand & Gamoran, 2003). It makes sense then that to improve teaching and learning, teachers would benefit from studying their everyday language use and nonverbal interactions in classrooms. Engaging in such analysis provides a robust method for reflecting and improving upon their practice (Juzwik & Ives, 2010), such as pinpointing specific interactional patterns that enable or prohibit them from enacting preferred teacher identities (Vetter et al., 2013). We borrow the term "interactionally aware" from Rex and Schiller (2009), who use it to describe teachers who are aware of the how talk impacts instruction and learning in their classroom. Such awareness opens opportunities for teachers to become more responsive to the diverse learning identities of students because they recognize that learning is shaped by multiple factors, such as personal relationships (de Freitas, 2008). Such awareness might also provide space for teachers to note that when learning identities are confined by classroom discourses, such as assumptions about what it means to be a "good" reader or writer, teachers can trouble those assumptions of what it means to be successful in school (de Freitas, 2008; Rex & Schiller, 2009).

We share Rex and Schiller's view that fostering interactional awareness is paramount to teacher learning and professional development. This book provides teacher educators and their students with support to build their interactional awareness by analyzing classroom interactions using video. Video as a medium is advantageous because it captures both language use *and* nonverbal communication as a means to support this work; video also allows a single event to be reviewed multiple times and used as a data source for analysis. To support and examine how student teachers undertake identity work as a means for building interactional awareness, we used positioning theory with discourse analysis (Davies & Harré, 1990). We found that these concepts used together help candidates become aware that the

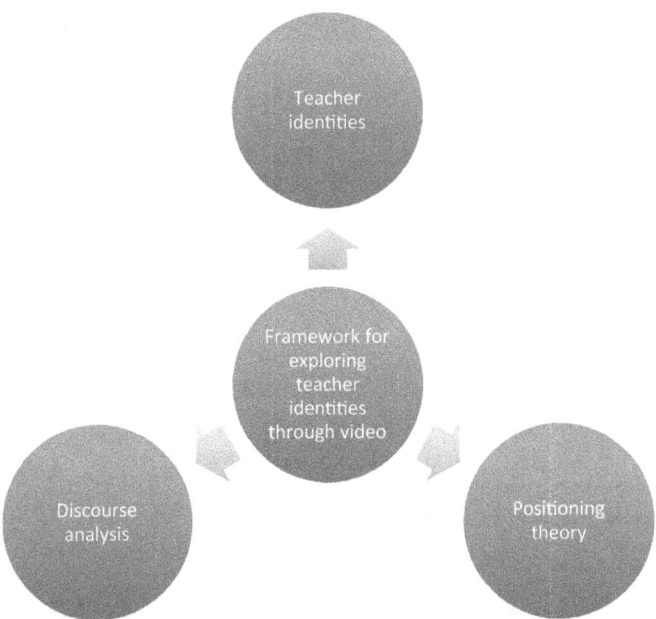

Figure 2.2 Framework for Exploring Teacher Identities through Video

structure and content of their talk and nonverbal actions relate to their identities and the way they are perceived by others (Rex & Schiller, 2009).

Positioning Theory

We view positioning theory as essential to our framework because it reveals how teachers construct and enact identities over time and in relation to their students and colleagues. We draw from the following definition of positionality: "The discursive process whereby selves are located in conversations as observably and subjectively coherent participants in jointly produced storylines" (Davies & Harré, 1990, p. 91). In other words, positionality is how people engage in conversation in ways that "take up or resist positions others create for them" (Rex & Schiller, 2009, p. 9). Within discursive interactions, individuals position themselves either interactively (i.e., when a person positions another person or is positioned by someone else) or reflexively (i.e., when a person positions themselves) (Davies & Harré, 1990). These first-order positionings may occur when a teacher situates a student as an engaged writer, and in turn that student may take up that position by reading their refined composition aloud to the class. Dependent on issues of power and status, positions can be resisted or taken up during interactions, and new positions can be created, both spontaneously and purposefully.

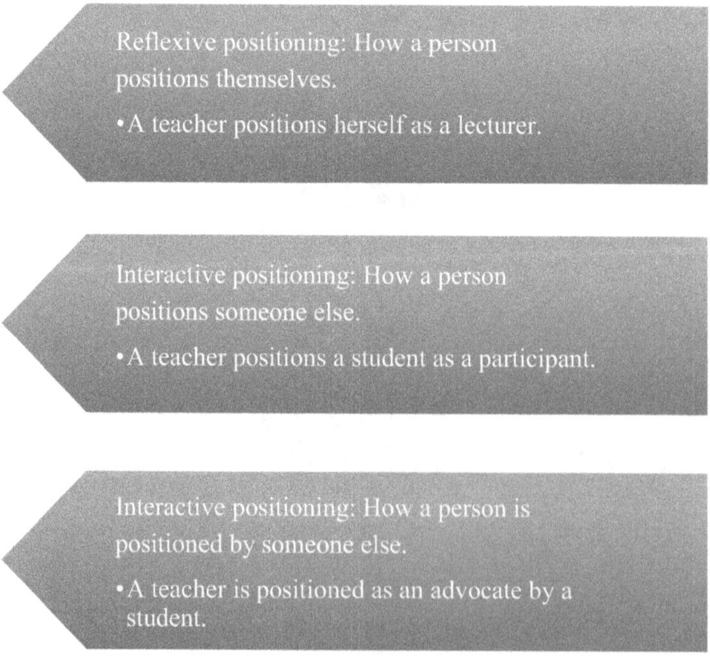

Reflexive positioning: How a person positions themselves.
- A teacher positions herself as a lecturer.

Interactive positioning: How a person positions someone else.
- A teacher positions a student as a participant.

Interactive positioning: How a person is positioned by someone else.
- A teacher is positioned as an advocate by a student.

Figure 2.3 Reflexive and Interactive Positionings

When a student resists that position of an engaged writer by refusing to write, second-order positioning occurs. Such challenges occur frequently in classroom interactions and they can reveal issues of power and status that might hinder learning. When individuals challenge first-order positionings within a separate discussion about the first conversation, third-order positionings occur. For instance, in a conversation with a cooperating teacher about a past interaction, a preservice teacher might reposition a student as a disengaged writer after noticing that they did not share their work in a small group read aloud. Third-order forms of positioning are considered to be descriptive, as they take place within talk or written discussion about past interactions. Students' analysis of transcribed interactions and interviews about those transcriptions are examples of third-order positionings.

Educational research has used positioning theory to investigate how teachers and students position themselves and others within classrooms (Clarke, 2006; Leander, 2002; Vetter, 2010). Such work illustrates how teachers intentionally or unintentionally situate students in ways that shape their learning and membership in a classroom community (Reeves, 2009; Wortham, 2004). The reflective and interactive positionings of teachers certainly shape instructional practices (e.g., writing process) and also students' access to identities (e.g., capable learner) (Reeves, 2009). For preservice teachers, the examination of how such positions occur during moment-to-moment interactions can be helpful because it opens occasions for them to examine their identity enactments over time. In other words, positioning and identity theory can help preservice teachers think critically and purposefully about how to "become" the kind of teachers they want to become and negotiate identities within specific contexts (Ma & Singer-Gabella, 2011). This book offers several examples for how positioning theory was used as a tool for self-analysis with preservice teachers. However, we realized that preservice teachers needed a method to access how they position themselves and their students. Thus, we taught them how to examine specific interactional moves using tools associated with discourse analysis as described below.

Teachers Studying Their Own Discourse: Why is it Important?

Discourse analysis is the study of how people use discourse (naturally occurring talk and other identity markers such as gestures or dress) to position themselves in strategic ways to belong to a particular social group. Moje and Lewis (2007) also refer to these social groups as discourse communities. Alternatively, discourse analysis may reveal that individuals position themselves in ways that are outside of the group's accepted norms, and thus struggle to find acceptance. A preservice teacher who identifies as a culturally responsive educator in a school that focuses on packaged curriculum and test preparation would struggle for acceptance in this situation; learning to speak back to powerful discourse communities and enact preferred teacher identities amid testing pressure is a frequent struggle for our teacher candidates.

Informed by classroom studies that demonstrate the importance of talk and social interaction to learning (Allington, 2002; Applebee et al., 2003; Bloome, Carter, Christian, Otto, & Shuart-Faris, 2004), we note that to improve teaching and learning, teachers need to study their everyday language use in classrooms. Juzwik et al. (2013) concede that the need for teacher candidates "to gain knowledge and experiential understanding of how discourse can shape teaching and learning" is a central problem in teacher education (p. 4). Whereas the aforementioned studies and others have focused on studying how classroom discourse impacts teaching and learning (Cazden, 2001; Dyson, 1993; Heath, 1983; Rex & McEachen, 1999, 2001, 2002; Wortham, 2004), we know of few studies that document teachers analyzing their own classroom discourse to examine and improve their practice. Rex and Schiller (2009) provide a practical text for both preservice and inservice teachers to analyze classroom interactions to improve instruction. Such work found that teachers and students benefitted from the being interactionally aware in their classrooms. In addition, Orland-Barak and Yinon (2007) conducted a study of how English as a Foreign Language (EFL) teachers in Israel examined a transcript and lesson artifacts from one full lesson during the student teaching experience. Using guiding questions from the course instructor, candidates examined their transcripts for patterns of turn-taking and interaction to note any gaps between what they think they did and what actually happened during the lesson. Candidates also identified their strengths and made suggestions about how to modify their future classroom discourse to improve teaching and learning. Findings from three case studies demonstrated that candidates noticed tendencies to dominate classroom discourse, articulated understandings about teachers' questioning practices, and used theory to analyze their discourse in generative ways. The authors suggest these findings "shed an optimistic light on the potential of novices to reflect at levels beyond 'what works in the classroom'" (p. 966). They also learned that the context of a course that supports the student teaching experience offered student teachers a safe learning environment for troubling classroom discourse from both an emotional and objective or analytical stance. Orland-Barak and Yinon also recommend that teacher candidates would benefit from analyzing their classroom discourse at multiple points over time to track patterns and observe changes.

A more recent study (Juzwik et al., 2013) demonstrates how video-based tools supported English teacher candidates to analyze their classroom interactions in order to more effectively implement dialogically organized instruction (DOI). Dialogically organized instruction can be characterized as open-ended, academic discourse where students develop questions and are the primary contributors to classroom talk. Juzwik and her colleagues at Michigan State University implemented and researched a pedagogical design they call Video-Based Response and Revision (VBRR) to understand the effectiveness of this approach on candidates' learning about DOI.

To participate in VBRR, candidates uploaded video clips of classroom discussion to a web-based platform and used Web 2.0 technologies to analyze their classroom interactions and support one another to move toward more dialogically organized modes of instruction. Key findings from their study support that "focusing on *key focal concepts* in teaching is a more powerful pedagogical use of video work than considering teaching practices *in general*" (p. 33, emphasis original). Thus, having candidates examine their classroom discourse through a particular lens (such as the focus on identity and positioning in this book) can improve teaching and learning in the classroom. This book meets a need for more empirical research about how novice teachers examine their own classroom discourse to improve their practice.

ANALYZING CLASSROOM DISCOURSE TO EXAMINE IDENTITY AND POSITIONING

Discourse analysis that fosters the investigation of both positioning and identities can help preservice teachers notice how and why they construct and enact particular identities during classroom interactions. With that information, teacher candidates can make informed decisions about how to communicate and position themselves and their students in ways that support their desired teaching identities. There exist numerous theories and methods related to studying classroom discourse (Rex & Green, 2007). For the purpose of using these tools with novice teachers, we borrowed elements of Gee's (2000) broader approach to discourse analysis. Gee's broader approach examines how everyday language practices (e.g., questions, pronouns, etc.) connect to larger ideologies and social groupings, or identities. This approach provided us, and our students, with the methodological tools to connect micro-level practices such as classroom dialogue to larger macro-level ideas that informed our candidates' desired identities (e.g., constructivism or a facilitator identity) (see Table 2.2). To modify the analytic process for preservice teachers, we presented candidates with a list of questions that prompted them to apply these analytic tools to the three video-recorded lessons without overwhelming them with theoretical and methodological constructs used by linguists and educational researchers (see Table 2.1). For an example, we provide information from the first video assignment. In this analysis, candidates selected a 5–10 minute clip to transcribe and focused primarily on the ways they used language and nonverbal communication to position themselves and their students.

Students examined their transcript and video clip for specific language use (e.g., teacher talk, open-ended questions) and made note of their nonverbal behaviors (e.g., standing at the front of the room). They then considered how these specific choices positioned them and their students in ways that either aligned or misaligned with their preferred teacher identities. Although there are many ways of studying classroom talk, we used positioning theory

Table 2.1 Questions From First Video Analysis Assignment

Video One
- Videotape an entire lesson of you facilitating learning in direct or indirect instruction. This can include a lecture, mini-lesson, discussion, and/or reading instruction.
- Transcribe 5–10 minutes of instruction, including both teacher and student talk.
- In a 2–3 page analysis, answer the following questions:
  - Who does the most talking?
  - What kinds of questions are posed? What kinds of answers are facilitated?
  - How do you talk to students? What is your tone? Do you use directives? Questions? Praises? Criticisms?
  - How do you think your words positioned your students as readers and writers? How do you think your students positioned you as a teacher? How did you position yourself as a teacher?
  - How might these positionings be shaped by how you were taught? By the kind of school you attended? By your race, class, gender, and/or sexual orientation?
  - What are the strengths? What will you do differently?
  - How did these positionings align (or not) with your desired teacher identities?

Table 2.2 Discourse Analysis Chart for Video-recorded Lesson

Number of lines of teacher talk
Number of lines of student talk
Number of closed questions
Number of open-ended questions
Describe teacher tone
Describe student tone
Number of general praises ("Good job.")
Number of specific praises ("It was helpful how you provided evidence to back up your claim.")
Number of general criticisms ("No, that's wrong.")
Number of specific criticisms ("Interesting claim. What evidence do you have to back it up?")

Juzwik et al. (2013)

because it helps to examine how preservice teachers construct and enact teacher identities during moment-to-moment interactions. For instance, many teacher candidates espoused constructivist theories they had been introduced to in their teacher education program that call for teachers to act as a facilitator of student learning. To examine their enactment of this desired identity, candidates analyzed if and how they asked open-ended questions to position students as knowledge builders and valued student input in their videos.

Try it Out: Explore Teacher Positions

To further illustrate these concepts, let's look at a brief transcript from one lesson in Hannah's classroom. As you read, take note of both reflexive and interactive positions. Use the following table to take notes.

As mentioned at the beginning of the chapter, this video-recorded and transcribed lesson took place in a tenth-grade honors English classroom. Hannah's objective was to facilitate discussion about heroic traits in an attempt to provoke interest in and build prior knowledge about Hercules. Before students discussed, she asked them to write down initial thoughts about the broad concepts they discussed in the conversation.

> **Hannah:** Okay . . . for number one. Can a person who has committed murder become a hero?
> **Hattie:** No.
> **Hannah:** Alright . . . why?
> **Hattie:** Because they've killed somebody! For like, okay . . . I mean, it depends on what their murder was. Which obviously, which I would think it would be like if they killed somebody for no apparent reason. So . . . they should not be allowed to be considered a hero.
> **Hannah:** Okay . . . so you're saying across the board, no.
> **Hattie:** Yes.
> **Hannah:** Okay . . . Corey. What do you think?
> **Corey:** Yes.
> **Hannah:** Yes? Okay. . .

Table 2.3 Analysis Chart for Reflexive and Interactive Positionings

Evidence from transcript or reflective statement (list transcript lines or describe interaction).	Reflexive Positioning: How did the teacher position his or herself?	Interactive Positionings: How did the teacher position students?	Interactive Positionings: How did students position the teacher?

Corey: Because . . . Moses killed an Egyptian before . . . So Moses killed an Egyptian and God chose Moses to lead the Israelites to the Promised Land. So obviously God found favor with Moses.

Hannah: Okay. . . let me throw a curveball, though. Doesn't *The Bible* also say, "Thou shalt not kill?"

Corey: Whoa! He was forgiven!

Hannah: He was forgiven? Okay then. Jamaal?

Jamal: I would say if he does it under reasonable circumstances. I mean, you shouldn't kill somebody for the fun of it. I mean, people do it. Reasonable circumstance, that's all I have to say for that one.

Hannah: Give me an example of a reasonable circumstance. What do you mean?

Jamal: Police officers. I mean, they're in a situation where they kill somebody that might kill them. I mean obviously the police officer is going to kill them, so like I said, reasonable circumstances.

Hannah: Like a kill or be killed kind of situation . . . okay. Kristen.

Kristen: I said yes, because like, well I mean there's people in prison who change the way they see things.

Hannah: We've all heard stories about people in prison for murder who, you know . . . did stupid things when they were young, were under the influence of drugs, who have completely reformed their lives. And sometimes, you know, it seems like they really mean it. So, it is kind of possible sometimes to change your ways. Alright . . . Harriet.

Harriet: Well, like with military people . . . they kill people for a living and they're considered to be heroes who are fighting for our country. So, people that kill people to protect others for the greater good. I think they could be considered heroes.

Hannah: Very good. Excellent.

From Hannah's teacher philosophy statement that she wrote for class, she stated that she valued classroom dialogue that is open and interactive. To align her teacher philosophy with classroom practice, Hannah would need to enact a facilitator teacher identity. To be a facilitator, one needs to pose open-ended questions and put students' responses into play with one another to construct a deeper conceptual understanding of a topic (Elizabeth, Anderson, Snow, & Selman, 2012; Juzwik, Borsheim-Black, Caughlan, & Heintz, 2013). To provide an example of this kind of analysis, we include our interpretation of Hannah's classroom interaction, followed by her own written analysis. At the end of the chapter, we provide guiding questions to promote reflection and discussion about your own thoughts in relation to this example.

We see several specific instances where Hannah's talk aligned with her enactment of a facilitator identity. For example, she began the discussion with an open-ended question that ties the reading to the concept of heroism ("Can a person who has committed murder become a hero?"). Her initial posing of this question positioned herself as a teacher who facilitates students' knowledge, rather than an authority on this topic. Thus, she also positioned her students as intellectually capable readers and thinkers about the topic at hand. In the next turn, a student, Hattie, replies "No," but does not offer an extended explanation for her answer. Rather than accept Hattie's limited response and fill the void with her own thoughts, Hannah pushed her to elaborate ("Alright . . . why?"). This interactional move positioned Hattie as a valued member of the discussion who is capable of contributing her own interpretation, rather than searching for the correct response for which the teacher already knows the answer. A few turns later in the transcript, Hannah built on Hattie's ideas by asking for another student perspective ("Okay Corey . . . what do you think?"). Here, Hannah positioned herself as a teacher who facilitates students' ideas and multiple perspectives. We also see that Hannah encouraged students to justify their responses with evidence. Next, when Jamal shared that there are reasonable circumstances that might lead one to commit murder, Hannah scaffolded his academic thinking by asking him to follow up with evidence ("Give me an example of a reasonable circumstance. What do you mean?"). Her directive placed the intellectual work on the student and positioned him as a capable student. Throughout the interaction, we witness students construct deeper understandings about the nuances associated with heroism and consider multiple contexts concerning police officers and the military that made this conversation messy and complex—the very markers of an academic discussion that research supports builds students' social and cognitive skills and academic language use (Applebee et al., 2003). Therefore, by strategically using language to position herself as a teacher who invites students' responses (and students as capable literacy learners), we see alignment of Hannah's teacher philosophy and her enactment of her desired facilitator identity.

Although Hannah positioned herself as a facilitator during this discussion, there were a few missed opportunities that are worth discussing. First, as a facilitator, it is important to capture the thoughts of the speaker, especially when repeating thoughts for the rest of the class. At the beginning of the excerpt, Hattie explained that a person cannot be considered a hero if they kill a person for no reason. Hannah repeated her thought by saying that Hattie believed that across the board, there is no way a person who killed someone could be considered a hero. We would argue that there was more complexity to Hattie's thought and the class might have benefitted from talking about the complexity. Second, at the very end of the excerpt, Hannah said, "Very good. Excellent." These praises were most likely meant to provide positive reinforcement to the students, however, they may be fostering the need for students to gain approval or affirmation from the teacher, a position that Hannah resisted in the opening reflection. One way that Hannah could offer praise that fosters more learning opportunities is by making her feedback more specific. In other words, she might have rephrased her comment to say, "That thought brings up an interesting point about how killing can be considered to be heroic by our society. What do others think of this point?" That way, the class would have the opportunity to understand why the point is worth praising and it opens opportunities for others to add their perspectives to the discussion. By discussing these missed opportunities, we do not mean to criticize Hannah's interactions, but instead facilitate growth in a teaching skill (facilitating discussions) that is extremely complex.

How does Hannah leverage these concepts to make sense of her classroom interactions? Next, let's see how Hannah applies the guiding questions focused on the nature of who does the talking, the kinds of questions that are posed, and the tone established for her first video analysis:

> From what I observed in my video, I think that there was a fairly good balance of students and teacher talk. Given that it was a class discussion that centered around the student's opinions/perceptions, I made sure that every student who had a statement to make was able to make his/her voice heard. I think that the students had ample opportunities to vocalize their opinions, and I likewise allowed myself a little time to reflect and respond to what the students were saying. I also made a connection between our class discussion and the readings we were about to begin. I think that the conversational, casual tone of the class discussion made for a good balance—from what I can tell, the students did just as much as, if not more, talking than I did, which I consider to be a good thing (as long as it's relevant to the lesson at hand).

Here, Hannah noticed a few classroom discourse patterns that supported her vision for the discussion. She noticed that the conversation was more student-centered than teacher-dominated and that she used her language to make sure students who wanted to contribute were heard. Also, she characterized the tone of the class discussion as "casual," which may have contributed to students taking more risk with sharing their ideas. Next, Hannah examined how her use of language positioned students as readers and writers and how she positioned herself as a teacher during this interaction.

> I think that my words positioned students as readers and writers by providing them with a "jumping off" point for the discussion concepts. After asking a question, I really let them take it up by writing about the issues and then allowing them to talk in a discussion. I think that allowing students that time to process really strengthens their analytic skills and their discussions as well. I position my students as having the power to incorporate their own opinions and experiences into the readings and discussions, which I feel really empowers my students. I think that my

students feel comfortable with and accept me as their teacher and as an authority figure. With that said, I think that my students also recognize that I hold them all accountable for their words and their actions. I think I've positioned myself as a laid-back teacher who loves student input and involvement, but requires some sense of order.

Hannah commented that she positioned her students as readers and writers through the use of discussion questions. Specifically, she observed that giving these questions to students and asking them to write down their initial thoughts before the discussion allows students the opportunities to analyze their thoughts in relation to a future reading. She also recognized that providing opportunities for students to voice their perspective in class is a way to push back against the traditional power relations between teacher as knower and learner as listener. Through the use of discussion questions, Hannah understood that her students situate her as someone with whom they can share their perspective (i.e., "comfortable"). Hannah stated that students also situated her as an authoritative figure who holds them accountable for their words and actions. Although we do not see evidence of Hannah managing behavior, the respectful dialogue from students and teacher could be evidence that students position her in that way. To end, she confirmed that she positioned herself as a laid-back teacher who invited dialogue and maintained order so that students could safely engage in conversation.

Does this align with her preferred teaching identities? Hannah addressed the assignment's guiding question to consider how these positionings might be informed by her own history of classroom interaction:

> I think that these positionings come chiefly from my educational background, to be honest. I was held to a very high standard as far as academics throughout my educational career, and I was very successful in my high school English classes. I've been trying very hard in my planning and in my student teaching to translate a lot of the positive experiences I had in my AP course into similar positive experiences in my own classroom. Part of that to me is creating an open environment and a strong classroom community where my students and I feel comfortable with one another. I think that the way I talk with my students has come out of years of feeling comfortable with my own teachers and paying careful attention to classroom dynamics even before I ever started student teaching.

Hannah observed that she adopted the ways she was positioned as a student by her own teachers in an Advanced Placement course as a resource for conducting her own classroom. Her own teachers positioned her as academically capable ("I was held to a very high standard"). The strategic ways she used language to create a casual classroom environment were informed by her own models of teacher and student interaction that she felt contributed to her positive growth and school and academic success. Therefore, Hannah was able to align the desired teacher identities she felt positively contributed to her identity as a student with how she enacted a facilitator identity in her own classroom. We recognize, however, that Hannah's own experience was not the only factor that opened opportunities for her to create an open and interactive classroom. Because she worked with students from similar backgrounds, she was able to quickly build rapport with them and students felt comfortable sharing opinions and experiences. This is not always the case when students and teachers come from different backgrounds, as we will discuss in chapter three.

Teachers typically depend on the use of particular discourse patterns for guiding, monitoring, and assessing the instruction they facilitate for their students (Edwards & Mercer, 1987; Mercer, 2000). Specifically, teachers use questions, recaps, elaborations, and reformulations as a way to foster discussion about a topic, summarize salient features of past events, clarify what has been said, and make connections to academic discourse of the curriculum (Lemke, 1990; Wells, 2000). These discourse patterns are most effective when teachers challenge students to give evidence for their statements, organize interactions and mutual support among students, and encourage students to actively participate in classroom events (Nassaji & Wells, 2000). Based on that information, we wondered if Hannah effectively used teacher talk to create an open and interactive classroom. What more could be done? Would you argue that students are constructing knowledge and negotiating meaning about heroic stances through this discussion? Why or why not?

EXPLORING THE FRAMEWORK IN PRACTICE

Using the tools of discourse analysis with video and transcripts to track positioning and identity, Hannah and other teacher candidates you will read about in this book were able to identify both instances of alignment and misalignment as they attempted to enact preferred teaching identities. We believe these analytic exercises provide novice, struggling, or even experienced teachers ways to improve their practice and ultimately increase student achievement and self-efficacy in school. In the remaining chapters of this book, we focus on different desired identities that student teachers in this study both adopted and struggled to enact, as described in chapter one.

REFERENCES

Allington, R.L. (2002). What I've learned about effective reading instruction. *Phi Delta Kappan, 83*(10), 740–747.
Alsup, J. (2006). *Teacher identity discourses: Negotiating personal and professional spaces*. Mahwah, NJ: Lawrence Erlbaum.
Applebee, A., Langer, J., Nystrand, M., & Gamoran, A. (2003). Discussion based approaches to developing understanding: Classroom instruction and student

performance in middle and high school English. *American Educational Research Journal, 40*(3), 685–730.
Anzaldua, G. (1999). *Borderlands-La Frontera: The New Mestiza*. San Francisco: Aunt Lute Books.
Beijaard, D., Meijer, P. C., & Verloop, N. (2004). Reconsidering research on teachers' professional identity. *Teaching and teacher education, 20*(2), 107–128.
Bloome, D., Carter, S. P., Christian, B. M., Otto, S., & Shuart-Faris, N. (2004). *Discourse analysis and the study of classroom language and literacy events: A microethnographic perspective*. New York: Routledge.
Bourdieu, P. (1991). *Language and symbolic power*. Cambridge, MA: Harvard University Press.
Bourdieu, P. (2011). The forms of capital. In I. Szeman & T. Kaposy (Eds.) *Cultural theory: An anthology*, (pp. 81-----93). Indianapolis, IN: Wiley-Blackwell.
Britzman, D. P. (1991). Decentering discourses in teacher education: Or, the unleashing of unpopular things. *Journal of Education, 173*(3), 60–80.
Britzman, D. P. (1994). Is there a problem with knowing thyself? Toward a poststructuralist view of teacher identity. In T. Shanahan (Ed.), *Teachers thinking, teachers knowing: Reflections on literacy and language education* (pp. 53–75). Urbana, IL: National Council of Teachers of English.
Butler, J. (1993). *Bodies that matter: on the discourse limits of "sex."* New York: Routledge.
Clarke, L. (2006). Power through voicing others: Girls' positioning of boys in literature circle discussions. *Journal of Literacy Research, 38*(1), 53–79.
Coldron, J., & Smith, R. (1999). Active location in teachers' construction of their professional identities. *Journal of curriculum studies, 31*(6), 711–726.
Cooper, K., & Olson, M. R. (1996). Chapter 7: The Multiple "I's" of Teacher Identity. In R. T. Boak, W. R. Bond, D. Dworet, & M. Kompf (Ed.), *Changing research and practice: Teachers' professionalism, identities, and knowledge* (p. 78). London, UK: RoutledgeFalmer.
Danielewicz, J. (2001). *Teaching selves: Identity, pedagogy, and teacher education*. Albany, NY: State University of New York Press.
Davies, B., & Harré, R. (1990). Positionings: The discursive production of selves. In B. Davies (Ed.), *A body of writing* (pp. 87–106). New York, NY: AltaMira Press.
Day, C. (Ed.). (1999). *Developing teachers: The challenges of lifelong learning*. Philadelphia, PA: Psychology Press.
DeCorse, C. J., & Vogtle, S. P. (1997). In a complex voice: The contradictions of male elementary teachers' career choice and professional identity. *Journal of Teacher Education, 48*(1), 37.
de Freitas, E. (2008). Troubling teacher identity: Preparing mathematics teachers to teach for diversity. *Teaching Education, 19*(1), 43–55.
Dyson, A. H. (1993). *Social worlds of children: Learning to write in an urban primary school*. New York: Teachers College Press.
Edwards, D., & Mercer, N. (1987). *Common knowledge*. New York: Routledge.
Elizabeth, T., Anderson, T., Snow, E., & Selman, R. (2012). Academic discussions: An analysis of instructional discourse and an argument for an integrative assessment framework. *American Educational Research Journal, 49*(6), 1214–1250.
Erikson, E. H. (1968). *Identity: Youth and crisis* (No. 7). New York: WW Norton & Company.
Fairbanks, C. M., Duffy, G. G., Faircloth, B., He, Y., Levin, B., Rohr, J., & Stein, C. (2010). Beyond knowledge: Exploring why some teachers are more thoughtfully adaptive than others. *Journal of Teacher Education, 61*, 161–171.
Florio-Ruane, S. (2002). More light: An argument for complexity in studies of teaching and teacher education. *Journal of Teacher Education, 53*(3), 205–215.

Freedman, S. W., & Appleman, D. (2008). "What else would I be doing?": Teacher identity and teacher retention in urban schools. *Teacher Education Quarterly,* 35(3), 109–126.

Gay, G. (2010). *Culturally responsive teaching.* New York: Teachers College Press.

Gee, J. P. (2000). Identity as an analytic lens for research in education. *Review of research in education,* 25, 99–125.

Gee, J. P. (2005). An introduction to discourse analysis theory and method (2nd ed). New York: Routledge.

Haniford, L. (2010). Tracing one teacher candidate's discursive identity work. *Teaching and Teacher Education,* 26, 987–996.

Heath, S. B. (1983). *Ways with words: Language, life and work in communities and classrooms.* Cambridge, MA: Cambridge University Press.

Holland, D., Skinner, D., Lachicotte, W., & Cain, C. (1998). *Identity and agency in cultural worlds.* Cambridge, MA: Harvard University Press.

Horn, I. S., Nolen, S. B., Ward, C., & Campbell, S. S. (2008). Developing practices in multiple worlds: The role of identity in learning to teach. *Teacher Education Quarterly,* 35, 61–72.

Juzwik, M. M., Borsheim-Black, C., Caughlan, S., & Heintz, S. (2013). *Inspiring dialogue: Talking to learn in the English Classroom.* New York: Teacher College Press.

Juzwik, M. M., & Ives, D. (2010). Small stories as resources for performing teacher identity. *Narrative Inquiry,* 20(1), 37–61.

Kerby, A. P. (1991). *Narrative and the self.* Bloomington: Indiana University Press.

Lave, J., & Wenger, E. (1991). *Situated learning: Legitimate peripheral participation.* Cambridge, UK: Cambridge University Press.

Leander, K. (2002). Locating Latayna: The situated production of identity artifacts in classroom interactions. *Research in the Teaching of English,* 37, 198–250.

Lemke, J. L. (1990). *Talking science: Language, learning, and values.* Norwood, NJ: Ablex Publishing Corporation.

Ma, J. Y., & Singer-Gibella, M. (2011). Learning to teach in the figured world of reform mathematics: Negotiating new models of identity. *Journal of Teacher Education,* 62(1), 8–22.

Mead, G. H., & Mind, H. (1934). *Self and society.* Chicago: University of Chicago Press.

Mercer, N. (2000). *Words and minds: How we use language together.* London: Routledge.

Mishler, E. G. (2004). Historians of the self: Restorying lives, revising identities. *Research in Human Development,* 1(1–2), 101–121.

Moje, E., & Lewis, C. (2007). Examining opportunities to learn literacy: The role of critical sociocultural literacy research. In C. Lewis, P. Enciso, & E. Moje (Eds.), *Reframing sociocultural research on literacy* (pp. 15–48). New York: Lawrence Erlbaum Associates.

Nassaji, H., & Wells, G. (2000). What's the use of 'triadic dialogue'?: An investigation of teacher-student interaction. *Applied linguistics,* 21(3), 376–406.

Orland-Barak, L., & Yinon, H. (2007). When theory meets practice: What student teachers learn from guided reflection on their own classroom discourse. *Teaching and Teacher Education,* 23(6), 957–969.

Pennington, J. L. (2007). Silence in the classroom/whispers in the halls: Autoethnography as pedagogy in White pre-service teacher education. *Race Ethnicity and Education,* 10(1), 93–113.

Reeves, J. (2009). Teacher investment in learner identity. *Teaching and Teacher Education,* 25(1), 34–41.

Rex, L. A. (2001). The remaking of a high school reader. *Reading Research Quarterly,* 36(3), 288–314.

Rex, L. A., & Green, J. L. (2007). Classroom discourse and interaction: Reading across the traditions. In B. Spolsky & F.M. Hult (Eds.), *International handbook of educational linguistics* (pp. 571–584). London: Blackwell.

Rex, L. A., & McEachen, D. (1999). "If anything is odd, inappropriate, confusing, or boring, it's probably important": The emergence of inclusive academic literacy through English classroom discussion practices. *Research in the Teaching of English*, 34(1), 65–129.

Rex, L. A., & Schiller, L. (2009). *Using discourse analysis to improve classroom interaction*. New York, NY: Routledge.

Ronfeldt, M., & Grossman, P. (2008). Becoming a professional: Experimenting with possible selves in professional preparation. *Teacher Education Quarterly*, 35, 41–60.

Sexton, D. M. (2008). Student teachers negotiating identity, role and agency. *Teacher Education Quarterly, Summer*, 73–88.

Sfard, A., & Prusak, A. (2005). Telling identities: In search of an analytic tool for investigating learning as a culturally shaped activity. *Educational Researcher*, 34(4), 14–22.

Sugrue, C. (1997). Student teachers' lay theories and teaching identities: Their implications for professional development. *European Journal of Teacher Education*, 20(3), 213–225.

Vaught, S. E., & Castagno, A. E. (2008). "I don't think I'm a racist": Critical Race Theory, teacher attitudes, and structural racism. *Race Ethnicity and Education*, 11(2), 95–113.

Vetter, A. (2010). Positioning students as readers and writers: An examination of teacher's improvised responses in a high school English classroom. *English Education*, 43(1), 33–64.

Vetter, A., Meacham, M., & Schieble, M. (2013). Leveling the field: Negotiating positions of power as a preservice teacher. *Action in Teacher Education*, 35(4), 230–251.

Vetter, A., Myers, J., & Hester, M. (2014). Negotiating ideologies about teaching writing in a high school English classroom. *The Teacher Educator*, 49(1), 10–27.

Vygotsky, L. S. (1978). *Mind and society: The development of higher mental processes*. Cambridge: Harvard University Press.

Weber, R. (1991). Linguistic diversity and reading in American society. *Handbook of Reading Research*, 2, 97–119.

Wells, G. (2000). Dialogic inquiry in education. In C. D. Lee & P. Smagorinsky (Eds.) *Vygotskian perspectives on literacy research: Constructing meaning through collaborative inquiry*. Cambridge, UK: Cambridge University Press.

Wortham, S. (2004). From good student to outcast: The emergence of a classroom identity. *Ethos*, 32(2), 164–187.

3   Positions of Power

In this chapter, we explore how one preservice teacher analyzed positions of power during his time as a student teacher. To begin, we provide a brief scenario. A few weeks into student teaching, Jay, a pseudonym for a preservice teacher in a ninth-grade English classroom, attempted to engage students in conversation about proper comma usage in a list. After asking students to read their lists, one student read his aloud. With chalk in hand, Jay began writing a series of inappropriate slang words in Spanish (e.g., *bésame culo*) that he did not understand. Although students laughed and added commentary to the list, Jasmine (a student) told Jay, "They got you cussin' and you don't even know it." These kinds of interactions were frequent for Jay, whose goal was to be a teacher who leveled "the playing field" in the classroom through dialogue and relevant curriculum. After this lesson, Jay reflected,

> I try to position my students and myself on an even field when it comes to writing, but where classroom management is concerned, I need to place myself above them as the authority. My students need to position me as someone who should be respected and listened to.

We start with this example not as a critique of Jay, but to illustrate how he struggled, as many novice teachers do, to negotiate positions of power. This was particularly difficult for Jay, who expressed a desire to construct and enact a critical pedagogy teacher identity that attempted to "level the field" for students by facilitating discussions that questioned power relations. Building on Freire's (2000) usage of this term, we define a critical pedagogue as a teacher who aims to dismantle traditional hierarchical roles between students and the teacher. Whereas the very structure of schooling creates these hierarchies through grading policies, for example, teachers who enact critical pedagogy identities do so in part by creating spaces for student voice and positioning themselves as engaging in knowledge building with students. These identity enactments are very difficult for novice teachers as they learn to balance traditional identities related to the teacher as authority figure with the desire to enact identities informed by critical pedagogy in the classroom. Although the data from Jay's story does not illustrate how he fostered dialogue about critical issues with students, he attempts to take on a critical pedagogy identity by dismantling traditional hierarchies between students and teacher.

For us, Jay's story raised questions about how his negotiations of power affected the ways in which he constructed his teacher identities. It was evident that if Jay was going to successfully engage in critical pedagogy, his preferred way of teaching, he needed to figure out how to negotiate positions of power with students. Specifically, this chapter illustrates how the assignment opened opportunities for Jay to reflect on the relationship between positions of power and identity enactment during moment-to-moment classroom interactions. To examine that dilemma in Jay's case, we asked the following questions:

- In what ways did Jay negotiate issues of power during his student teaching?
- How did those negotiations shape his identity constructions and enactments of his desired teacher identities of a critical pedagogue?
- In what ways did video analysis of three lessons engage Jay in reflection about his negotiations of power?

EXPLORING POSITIONS OF POWER

To begin, we discuss what we mean by positions of power and how this topic has been discussed in teacher education. We define *power* as interpersonal and dynamic. Thus, positions of power are constituted through discourse and accepted forms of knowledge (Foucault, 1979). Furthermore, we draw from Foucault's concept that power is not only a negative or repressive tool used for coercion. In other words, individuals are also capable of being powerful and powerless at the same time (Davies & Harré, 1990) and oftentimes use power in empowering ways. Specifically, a poststructuralist view of power suggests that individuals have the ability to change themselves and the world around them (i.e., agency) (Jackson, 2001).

During student teaching, preservice teachers are expected to negotiate positions of power with several individuals, such as cooperating teachers. By *negotiate* we mean when individuals try to reach a compromise with others. These power dynamics often serve to position teacher candidates in ways that may challenge their understanding of who they are as educators. Just as teachers may position their students as passive receivers of knowledge (Freire, 2000), preservice teachers' supervisors may also position them similarly. Thus, a tension may exist between their preferred teacher identity and the one that affords their entrance into a school (Assaf, 2005).

Cummins (2009) reminds preservice teachers that they have choices about how they negotiate power, thus reifying the concept that student teachers can take up positions of power. For example, those choices are expressed through language in how they interact with students, engage them cognitively, or activate their prior knowledge. Power, then, is created and shared between students in varying degrees. Interactions may contribute to disempowerment, or interactions might constitute a process of empowerment that challenges power dynamics. In other words, teachers might hint at or justify certain rules or content to yield compliance from students in a classroom (Puvirajah, Verma, & Webb, 2012). Such use of language has the potential to create a power-share or power-control classroom space. Although students do not hold structural power, they can situate themselves in positions of power as individuals and collectives, as seen in the opening example with Jay. Such positions might be enacted through resistance, oftentimes consisting of subtle moments, such as grumbling or sarcasm. To address those resistances and meet learning objectives, teachers must negotiate positions of power with students. Recognizing that negotiation occurs in the classroom implies that all participants have power. Thus, understanding and reflecting on reciprocal power negotiations is essential to understanding the construction and enactment of teacher identities, including current classroom practices, and should be a part of teacher education curriculum (Jackson, 2001). This was particularly important for Jay, who struggled to negotiate more leveled positions of power with students. Positions of power, then, affect how preservice teachers construct and enact teacher identities.

Negotiating Power in the Classroom

Several noteworthy studies (e.g., Agee, 2004; Alsup, 2006; Assaf, 2005; Handsfield, Crumpler, & Dean, 2010) have addressed how power affects the construction of teacher identities. In particular, these studies highlight the multiple and dynamic negotiations that preservice teachers deal with daily. For example, Agee (2004) explored how one teacher attempted to negotiate the power structure of high-stakes teaching as an early-career teacher and how those negotiations shaped her identity as a culturally relevant teacher. The study suggested that the teacher would have benefitted from a teacher education program that prepared her for how to navigate the constraints of the power structures related to high-stakes exams that are prominent in today's schools. Other studies (e.g., Jackson, 2001; Smagorinsky, Cook, Moore, Jackson, & Fry, 2004) point to power dynamics between cooperating teachers and student teachers and illustrate how frustrating tensions take a toll on feelings of control during the student teaching experience.

Teachers also negotiate power with students during classroom interactions. For instance, Juzwik's (2006) concept of the authoritative teacher suggests that such teachers continually negotiate positions with students in a dialogic way rather than presenting authoritarian static positions with which students must comply. An authoritative teacher, then, is one who is able "to persuade students to trust, respect, and learn from one's voice" without abusing the power of their authority (p. 490). Jay's earlier narrative about respecting students' voices while simultaneously earning their respect as a knowledgeable other in the classroom resembles Juzwik's construct. Similarly, Buzzelli and Johnston (2001) found that one teacher used a "soft power" approach rather than a heavy-handed approach when responding to inappropriate subject matter. In other words, she did not situate herself as an authoritarian by forbidding certain language from a student, but instead used her authority as a teacher to convey her concern and foster dialogue about the issue. Overall, teachers constantly negotiate positions of power during moment-to-moment interactions. Those negotiations affect how teachers and students enact their identities over time.

Teachers who focus on maintaining power over what counts as knowledge, however, are likely to meet resistance from students (Brooke, 1987; Linehan & McCarthy, 2000). With this approach, teachers situate themselves as knowledgeable, and student's learning takes on the game of guessing the right answer. Such positionings maintain traditional teacher and student power hierarchies. For instance, Gutierrez, Rymes, and Larson (1995) called the teacher talk in their study a "primary script" and student talk a "counterscript." Students sometimes asserted local popular knowledge (i.e., music) that was not taken up by the teacher script that undercut the roles expected of students. When this local knowledge was explicitly connected with the primary script, dialogic talk occurred in which teacher and students co-constructed knowledge in the classroom.

Preservice teachers also negotiate positions of power in ways that enable them to construct preferred teacher identities. Studies suggest several ways of promoting those opportunities, such as interviewing teachers about practice and developing learning communities between cooperating teachers, student teachers, and supervisors (Ritchie, Rigano, & Lowry, 2000). Within these communities, positions of power can be problematized and members feel more comfortable engaging in constructive conversations. Other suggestions include the telling of stories and dialogic narratives within a community of practice (Rogers, Marshall, & Tyson, 2006; Watson, 2006), using specific types of language to create power-share interactions (Puvirajah et al., 2012), and recontextualizing discourses across various school spaces to make changes within schools and teacher identities (Handsfield et al., 2010). Less research has examined how video analysis could be used as a tool for preservice teachers to analyze and reflect on positions of power during interactions.

Jay's Desired Teaching Identities: Power-Share

Although all of our students struggled to negotiate power to some degree, Jay struggled the most because of his desire to implement critical pedagogy in a school focused on skill-and-drill test practice. We believe that his case study could offer insight into how one preservice teacher put theory into practice within the context of an urban school. Jay, a White middle-class male in his early twenties, positioned himself as a lover of popular culture and a poet/writer. In several of his blog posts (completed for a course assignment), he shared his own poems and commented on his desire to write creatively. For a project that required students to present on a professional text, he chose to read *Getting the Knack* by Stephen Dunning and William Stafford and stated that, "I would really like for poetry to be a major part of my classroom, including providing the opportunity for students to write it." This is important because it is through his positioning of himself and his students as poets/writers that he seeks to, as he said, "level the field" within the classroom.

Jay also positioned himself as a teacher who hoped to implement aspects of critical pedagogy, such as facilitating dialogue that questioned power relations (Kellner, 2000). Jay reflected this perspective in his teaching philosophy when he stated, "I want to instill tolerance.... When critical thinkers are questioned they do not simply regurgitate what has been fed them, but offer a better question and possible solution." He wanted to "level the field" by taking on a dialogic approach that sought to rebalance preexisting power structures (Freire, 2000) and valued a perspective that pushed against viewing students as passive learners (Giroux, 2000).

Jay completed 50 hours of internship and 12 weeks of student teaching over the year at Carter High School (CHS). Carter High School is located in a city 20 miles from the university; this city has a population of 51,577. The total enrollment of CHS during Jay's preservice teaching experience was 795. Sixty-four percent of the students at this school were eligible for free and reduced lunch, compared to 34% in the state as a whole. The ethnicity of students at CHS in 2011 was 53% African American, 35% Latina/o, and 11% White. Fifty-three percent of students passed the comprehensive English exam (reading and writing skills) for the state (state average: 70%). Jay's preservice teaching experience took place in a ninth-grade English classroom with students between ages 14 and 17. Jay's students were predominantly Latino/a and spoke Spanish and English. His cooperating teacher was a young, White female who had been teaching fewer than 10 years. She typically took a teacher-centered approach in a school that highly emphasized success on high-stakes testing. This emphasis was due to state pressures to perform and compete with other schools across the district and state.

POSITIONS OF POWER

Jay's video assignment demonstrated that he negotiated positions of power with students in ways that enabled and prohibited his ability to construct and enact his preferred teacher identities. To illustrate those negotiations, we organize our findings in two major sections that identify areas of identity alignment and misalignment. First, we analyze a transcribed classroom interaction from the video assignment that portrays how Jay negotiated positions of power in ways that enabled him to situate himself as a critical pedagogue (i.e., power-share identity). Within that same section, we examine how he negotiated positions of power in his written analysis of the transcription to illustrate how the assignment did or did not help him negotiate positions of power. Second, we follow the same organization as above to highlight a transcribed classroom interaction and written analysis to illustrate how Jay attempted to negotiate positions of power in ways that prohibited him from situating himself as his desired identity (i.e., power-control identity).

Power-Share Identity

Classroom interaction. Jay hoped to enact a teacher identity informed by critical pedagogy, but when attempting to put it into practice he found he had to negotiate power in ways that allowed him to assert his authority while also "leveling the field." This was evident in Jay's first video analysis assignment, in which he filmed the eleventh-grade honors class responding to a journal topic about their favorite poem they read during the poetry unit. Jay stood at the front of the room and students sat in rows, an arrangement preferred by his cooperating teacher. He described this group to be "very quiet" and "well-behaved" and noted that with this group of students he was able to successfully negotiate power in ways that enabled him to construct his preferred teacher identity as a critical pedagogue. At the beginning of the lesson, Jay explained that they were going to review their poetry unit by discussing their favorite poems so far. First, students wrote responses, then Jay opened it up for a whole-group discussion. While discussing poems, such as "Favorite Color" or "Jabberwocky," a student directed the discussion toward his journal:

Wayne: Can we read our journals?
Jay: Yea.
Wayne: My favorite poem we have read so far is Mr. Talbot's (Jay's) poem about the writer. Mostly, I liked Mr. Talbot's imagination while writing it. It spoke to me because I could imagine his poem in my mind and in my imagination. It gave me a cool feeling because I would have thought and said some of the same things Mr. Talbot had mentioned.
Jay: Thank you, I appreciate that very much. I read my poem because I didn't want you guys to feel like, *who is this guy asking us to read our poetry in front of the whole class?* I thought it would be fair if I read something too. I always feel like if I ever take a creative writing class, I took one in college, and our teacher was a writer trying to get published and he would bring his stuff in and read it to the class. I found it inspiring and it was enjoyable because he was a really good writer. Does anyone else want to share?

At the beginning of this transcript, Wayne asked Jay if he could read rather than talk about his journal entry. By asking Jay if he could do this, Wayne situated Jay as the teacher and himself as a student by abiding by Jay's rules. By asking a question rather than throwing out an answer, Wayne complied with the typical storyline of how an academic conversation works (i.e., teacher is in charge and student complies). Jay informally answered "Yea" and took up a position of authority. By using informal language, however, he privileged informal discourse and attempted to "level the field." This positioned him as a power-sharing teacher by negotiating how the classroom conversation worked. Next, Wayne stated that he preferred Mr. Talbot's poem, thus situating Jay as teacher and writer. By using *Mr. Talbot*, he illustrated his belief that Jay is a teacher, a position he respected. Next, Wayne stated that he liked the poem because of Mr. Talbot's imagination and he could relate to what Jay wrote. In this scenario, Wayne constructed his reading and writing identities by giving specific examples related to why he liked Jay's poem (e.g., "I could imagine his poem"). Also, his use of the words *thought* and *said* indicated that Wayne wrote about similar topics or in similar structures, thus aligning himself with the teacher.

Jay's response attempted to construct a socially recognized identity of a democratic teacher. By using polite discourse (e.g., "Thank you") to negotiate power with the student, he illustrated his belief that student feedback was important and welcomed. Thus, Jay attempted to construct the politics of the classroom by portraying what kinds of interactions (democratic) were valued. Next, he elaborated by explaining that he wrote and read aloud his own poetry to them because he did not want them asking, "Who is this guy asking us to read our poetry in front of the whole class?" In this example, Jay followed the reading of his work with a discussion of his experience as a college student. He used the words *fair, inspiring,* and *enjoyable* to describe his ideal classroom. In this instance Jay's use of the words *this guy* positioned himself as less of an authority and as more of an everyday person who needed to earn his authority, despite his teacher position. He then explained to students that he believed it was only "fair" if he "read something too." By explaining his rationale, Jay attempted to situate himself as a former student and a writer and thus align part of his enacted teacher identities with his current students' identity positions. Jay's narrative about his personal experience explicitly discussed his positions as teacher, student, and writer with students, thus enacting a socially recognized power-share identity. Rather than stopping the conversation with the spotlight on Jay, he asked students if they wanted to continue sharing. As a result, the dialogue about poetry continued.

Jay's reflection. To understand how Jay made sense of these negotiations of positions of power, we examined an excerpt of his first video analysis assignment:

> I feel that I positioned students on an even playing field with their writing. I have encouraged all of them to write and have shown them that writing is messy and it takes time to develop. I have let them critique my

own poems so they feel like we are all working together. I have noticed with this class they give me a lot of respect as a teacher and authority figure . . . they seem to desire and value my feedback on their creative works. I have tried to be as validating as possible and give positive criticism of their work. For instance, when Will talked about a comment I gave him on his poem, he said I "tore it apart." I explained to him my comments and what I was trying to do. I also told him that he had the power over my comments by choosing to ignore them or use them.

Jay began this analysis by positioning himself as a teacher using writing instruction to create "an even playing field." To do this, he used "teacher talk" ("writing is messy," "value my feedback") to construct a socially recognized identity as a knowledgeable and experienced writing teacher. He also used "writer talk" ("critique my own poems") to position himself as a writer who valued feedback from his students. By using the words "give positive criticism" and "working together," he engaged in discourses that illustrated his ideological belief that teachers should situate themselves as writers and encourage student feedback in an attempt to create a student-centered curriculum and a writing community. By doing this, he attempted to construct a teacher identity that promoted a democratic classroom and to build classroom politics that valued the negotiation of power with students in ways that created a community of writers.

He also stated that students positioned him with respect because of his "teacher" actions, such as critical feedback and validation. To elaborate, Jay offered an example of student interaction with Will, who told Jay that he tore apart his work. At first, this statement appeared to contradict his earlier discussion about validation and positive criticism. However, Jay attempted to situate Will as a writer on an even playing field by discussing power dynamics between writer and teacher/editor. In other words, he explicitly described the typical storyline of a writer/editor relationship while reassuring Will that he has the power to make whatever changes he sees fit. We understand that Will may not take up this position, especially because his grade is dependent on Jay's feedback. We applaud Jay's attempt, however, to not only provide feedback to Will, as many teachers do, but also explain it in a way that relates to real-world interactions.

To further explain his approach, he stated:

> I position my students in the same way I have been positioned in college. I can position them in a more equal field because I do not worry about discipline problems. . . . I feel that students learn more when they are part of the discussion, working through their thinking with guidance, rather than just empty containers being "filled" by the teacher.

To begin, Jay used reflective language to state that his recent college experiences as a learner ("equal field") shaped how he constructed his teacher identity. He attributed this position to no behavior problems in the classroom. Through phrases, such as "learn more when they are part of," Jay privileged discussion over direct teaching and illustrated his preference to situate himself as a guide. Thus, Jay took up discourses that alluded to his belief in negotiating power with students to create a democratic classroom in which students are active participants.

With that said, Jay's phrase "even playing field" uncovers several dilemmas related to power negotiations. First, this phrase most likely illustrates Jay's attempt to construct classroom politics that even out barriers so that students can accomplish the same thing without being jeopardized by the limitations of the field (i.e., classroom). These discourses aligned with his teaching philosophy about his desire to practice critical pedagogy and relates to a power-share perspective. His use of that phrase also privileges knowledge about how education is a great equalizer, uncovering room for learning more about how disadvantaged backgrounds affect the success of students. We wondered about his thoughts in relation to student/teacher relationships, student needs, and student backgrounds. If Jay does not think about those aspects of pedagogy, he could possibly create a power-control space, despite his intentions to do the opposite. Finally, Jay clearly has assumptions about what make a "good and behaved" student. This perspective needs to be broadened in order to position students in the classroom as valued participants.

Power-Control Identity

Classroom interaction. Although Jay was able to enact his preferred identity as a power-share teacher, he tended to take on power-control positions when he met resistance from students. For example, in each of the three video segments, Jay positioned himself physically at the front and engaged in an IRE discourse pattern. During these sequences, very few students were engaged (i.e., lack of verbal and nonverbal participation) and little to no higher-level thinking was occurring (i.e., recalling characters and events from literature). Although reviewing factual information can be a useful part of lessons, Jay was not enacting the teacher identity described in his blogs. For instance, in Jay's second video transcription, he positioned himself as the knowledge-keeper when he and students discussed the novel *To Kill a Mockingbird*. Jay provided a chart in which the students were instructed to record short passages that demonstrated certain characters' personality traits.

> **Jay:** In your chart, what did we learn from Bob Ewell when Mr. Gilbert is talking?
> **Juan:** That he said that he saw, uh . . .
> **Jay:** [interrupts] that he saw Tom Robinson, he saw Tom Robinson raping May Ella, right? This is what we learned Mr. Gilbert [trails off]. That's what you should write in that little block . . . "We learned from Mr. Gilbert that Bob Ewell saw Tom Robinson . . . chased him off, but he saw him committing the act . . . he saw him raping May Ella."

Damien: Naw, that's what he said to Mr. Gilbert.
Jay: That's what he said to Mr. Gilbert, in the first block. That's what you should write.

In this example, Jay attempted to assess student comprehension of the chapter. He began with an open-ended question ("What did we learn?") and used the pronoun *we* to construct classroom politics that situated students as part of a reading community. The exchange shifted, however, when Juan appeared to have difficulty answering the question. Like many novice teachers, Jay answered his own question and interrupted the students' comment, rather than posing more questions or practicing a longer wait time, thus privileging teacher knowledge. As a result, students wrote down Jay's interpretation rather than their own. In the last few sentences, Damien contributed by saying, "Naw, that's what he said to Mr. Gilbert," potentially taking on the identity of a reader and participant. Jay then validated the comment by restating it and directing students to write down that statement. Despite Jay's desire to situate himself as a teacher who facilitated dialogue, Jay used a traditional IRE interaction, thus reflecting a power-control identity. At this point, Jay had difficulty negotiating positions of power with students when they did not follow his expected storyline of how a classroom should work (e.g., student participation).

As the lesson progressed, students and teacher continued to take on power-control positions resulting in an unsuccessful lesson. In the following segment, Jay taught a mini lesson on comma usage and asked students to create a sentence that used commas to set off a list. Students remained in their seats and Jay stood at the front. Josue volunteered his answer.

Josue: Chapa likes long, hard . . . [His voice falls when he says this word. He smiles.]
Jay: Who wants to share their journal, one sentence?
Josue: [Raises his hand.] I got one mister. [Jay erases the board, then turns around.]
Jay: Sure.
Josue: [Reads] "Today, Jumax, Chapa, and Playboy went to Manny's house." [Laughter.]
Jay: [Writes on board] "Today, Humax." [He points to Humax and looks at Josue.]
Josue: [Making a J form in the air with his finger.] Jumax. Like the juice.
Jay: Like the juice, what? [Puts his hands down to his sides palms outward.]
Josue: J, the j.
Jasmine: I seen that word be on that can don't it?
Jay: [Writes and says] Chapa. [Many students laugh.]
Jasmine: They got you cussin' and you don't even know it.
Student off camera: And puto! [Students laugh. Jay catches on and erases the board.]

Jasmine: Say, besamé culo! Put besamé culo up there. [Jay asks for more examples. Note: "Besame culo" is a common phrase in Spanish that generally means, "Kiss my ass."]

Jasmine: Ooo, oo, I got one. Yesterday, I went to go put fish food in my fish tank. [Note: This is a slang expression that references sexual intercourse. Students laugh.]

Second student off camera: That's not funny. That's nowhere near funny.

Jasmine: Then why are they laughing?

Second student off camera: They laughing at you they're not laughing at . . .

Third student off camera: I got a big fish tank. You know you got to lay on your side.

Jay: [Stops writing the sentence.]: Stop it. Guuuys! I do not care about the fish.

This transcript begins with Josue taking on the identity of a class comedian ("Chapa likes long, hard . . . ") by using inappropriate language that resists "school talk" and elicits laughter from classmates. For us (non-Spanish speakers) the word *chapa* was difficult to define because it has different meanings within different cultural contexts. In these instances when we could not determine the meaning of specific words, we went back to the video to capture the speaker's inflection and how other students reacted to its usage. Two Spanish-speaking colleagues from Cuba and Guyana, and three Spanish-speaking students from Mexico and El Salvador could not pinpoint the slang usage of *chapa*. Two urban dictionaries defined the word differently (i.e., a male prostitute or a lock on a door). Regardless of the exact meaning, it was clear that Josue implied a negative connotation that was inappropriate within traditionally defined teacher-student discourse. Jay's choice to ignore Josue's comments can be interpreted multiple ways. Based on his status as a novice teacher, however, Jay most likely did not know how to deal with Josue's inappropriate comment. He attempted to redirect the conversation back to an academic conversation by asking students to share their journals. This open-ended question could be interpreted as his attempt to open dialogue that facilitated a power-share interaction.

Josue's response ("I got one, Mister") at first glance illustrated his attempt to situate himself as a participant of the academic conversation. Perhaps Jay's redirection worked. However, Josue's use of *Mister*, rather than Jay's name, indicated how Josue distances himself from Jay. It appeared that to Josue, Jay was just another teacher that he does not trust. In response, Jay answered, "Sure" to facilitate more responses. Josue then read an inappropriate sentence ("Jumax, Chapa, and Playboy . . . ") to elicit laughter, construct solidarity between classmates, and disrupt academic norms. Thus, Josue attempted to resist privileged ways of knowing and behaving in the classroom by engaging in an inappropriate interaction.

Next, Jay attempted to write the sentence on the board, illustrating his lack of knowledge behind the meaning of Josue's sentence. We perceive Jay's attempt to situate Josue as a socially recognized participant of the academic conversation by writing his comment on the board. He also situated Josue as an expert by asking him how to spell the Spanish word. By doing this, Jay attempted to build classroom politics that encouraged students to be authorities. Josue responded by verbally and nonverbally telling Jay how to spell the word. He also said "like the juice" to provide context for Jay and perhaps build on background knowledge that Jay does not have. Jay illustrated his ignorance about Jumax verbally and nonverbally by asking, "Like the juice, what?" and making gestures with his palms. Josue made it simple, by stating, "J" and Jasmine aligned herself with Josue by saying, "I seen that word be on that can don't it?" Her sentence could be interpreted as an attempt to help Jay understand the word. At the same time, her (an African American female) sentence aligned herself with Josue and other Spanish-speaking students in the room. In a sense, Josue and Jasmine's comments created even more of a barrier between Jay and his students. They appear to be taking up discourses that say, "See how much you don't know about us" or, "We are not convinced that you are our teacher."

Jay then wrote *chapa* on the board, which elicited laughter from students and situated Jay as a nonauthority. Jasmine attempted to disrupt this kind of talk by interpreting the situation for Jay ("They got you cussin' and you don't even know it"). At the same time, her humorous tone indicated that she also wanted her classmates to know that she understood what they were doing. Again, she aligned herself with her classmates and joined in, further distancing herself from Jay. Thus, Jasmine used discourse that attempted to build and deconstruct accepted notions of what counts in a classroom. At this point, Jay appeared to catch on and erased *chapa* from the board. Jasmine, however, continued to use slang ("fish food") in ways that situated herself as a socially recognized comedian and elicited laughter from her classmates. At this point, Jay caught on and attempted to stop the inappropriate and disruptive talk with demanding statements. Jay's command ("Stop it") and exclamatory tone ("Guuuys!") situated students' comments as inappropriate, alluding to privileged types of interactions in the classroom, and illustrated his desire to redirect the conversation in another direction. By doing this, Jay continued to take on a socially recognized power-control identity that contrasted with his desired teacher identity and constructed classroom politics that discounted student participation.

Jay's reflection. To explore how video analysis helped Jay analyze his negotiations of power, we examined his response to the classroom interaction above. Jay wrote the following:

> I want to use discussion as much as possible in my teaching. I try to be as inclusive as possible. . . . One of the biggest issues I face is the language barrier. For most of my students English is their second language. . . . I try to make the environment as safe and uncritical as possible. I include

> discussing journals as part of a way to help them. Once they have their thoughts organized on paper they can more easily verbalize them to the class. . . . I have found some students resistant and defiant to my presence. Sometimes when I am up front speaking they will try to compete for the attention of the class. Josue is one of the most prominent students to do this. . . . He often tries to get everyone laughing, usually at the expense of another student. . . . I would like to handle off-topic conversations and critical comments towards each other better.

In this excerpt, Jay expressed his desire to facilitate more discussion in his classroom. Jay took up discourses that attempted to construct a socially recognized teacher identity that was "as inclusive as possible" and who tried "to make the environment as safe and uncritical as possible." To Jay, in this sense, leveling the field meant remaining open to student differences. At this point, he used reflective language ("figure out," "biggest issues I face") to examine his privileged notions of what inclusive, safe, and uncritical looks like in this context with students who have different cultural and linguistic backgrounds than his. He uncovered the possibility that the "language barrier" could be one reason why discussion was not successful and used teacher discourses to describe how he modified instruction for second language learners ("thoughts organized on paper"). In the second paragraph, Jay noted that some students, particularly Josue, resisted his position as a teacher by taking on comedic positions that disrupted the order of the classroom. Jay then used reflective teacher talk ("handle off-topic conversations") to list areas of improvement for the future.

In the same reflection we opened with in this chapter, Jay continued:

> I try to position my students and myself on an even field when it comes to writing, but where classroom management is concerned, I need to place myself above them as the authority. My students need to position me as someone who should be respected and listened to. I feel they do not see me as a "real" teacher because I am a "student teacher." I feel that in order for me to be the teacher that I plan to be, I need to get my classroom management under control so I can accomplish all of the things I want to do.

Jay stated that he needed to get his "classroom management under control" so he could "accomplish all of the things [he] want[ed] to do." He uses reflective language about interactive positionings ("students need to position me as someone who should be respected . . . ") to raise questions and alternative discourses about how to navigate these positions of power. He appears to be asking, "How can I take on a power-share position when students resist that position?" As a result, he stated that his students did not recognize his identity as a "real teacher." This reflection is important because Jay noted how students position him and he wrestles with ideas about how to change that positioning so that he can construct his preferred teaching identities.

Jay, however, had difficulty identifying the various layers of power structures and developing solutions to negotiate them in ways that favored his goals. Despite the inappropriate comments spoken in his classroom, Jay's only mention of this kind of interaction in his reflection was one sentence saying, "I do not speak Spanish so I cannot understand them." His reflection focused on how he should modify his actions to manage his classroom better rather than asking questions about why students resisted. Perhaps students resisted because Jay implemented a lesson that did not connect to their lives. This could be a result of the cultural and linguistic differences that exist between students and teacher. Jay, and most of the other students in his education class, did not discuss how his identity and culture (e.g., language and race) shaped interactive positionings and constructed identities in the classroom, even though he was asked to do so. His hesitation to observe these broader issues is typical of novice teachers and can relate to what Larson and Irvine (1999) called reciprocal distancing, in which teachers do not take up students' linguistic and cultural knowledge as resources in literacy learning. Although it was Jay's intent to be inclusive, he did not know how to gain respect from students when he was clearly not a member of their world. We recognize that as a novice teacher, Jay is most likely focused on reaching the goal of his lesson and understandably has a difficult time engaging in a critical analysis of how his culture and language shaped negotiations of power. For us, this signals an area in which Jay needed more support. With that support, such reflections could lead to a revision of what counts in a classroom, including the kinds of knowledge that are privileged.

FINAL THOUGHTS

Jay's blog referenced a phrase from Walt Whitman's *Song of Myself*, "Behold I do not give lectures or a little charity, When I give I give myself," to illustrate his desire to be true to himself in the classroom. This desire was what he struggled with the most. For Jay, his ability to take on his preferred teacher identity depended on how he negotiated positions of power with students. This study illustrated how the video analysis assignment opened opportunities for Jay to reflect on the relationship between those positions of power and identity enactment during moment-to-moment classroom interactions. By combining Sherin and van Es's (2009) notion of taking notice through video analysis and Rex and Schiller's (2009) challenge to reflect about power and identity through discourse analysis of classroom interactions, this study makes a significant impact on research about how teacher education programs can use video analysis to help preservice teachers analyze issues of power, positioning, and identity.

Specifically, the analysis challenged Jay to study how he positioned himself as a teacher, how students positioned him, and how he positioned students during classroom interactions. In addition, the close analysis of transcripts expected that Jay compare those enactments to his teaching philosophy and to critically think about how positions of power affected those enactments, including how he practiced critical pedagogy. As stated in the findings, Jay examined the impact of his interactions at a local level. For example, Jay justified how his talk and behavior aligned with his preferred teaching identity in the first section in findings. He discussed specific examples related to how he leveled the field ("I let them critique my poems") and explained his response to a student's comment ("tore it apart"). Clearly, Jay examined how he enacted his preferred teacher identity by referencing specific moments within the transcripts and videos. Having a transcript to go back to, as suggested by Rex and Schiller (2009), provided Jay with specific evidence rather than abstract talk about putting theory (critical pedagogy) into practice (Mosley, 2010).

In addition, Jay also reflected about how his difficulty negotiating positions of power impacted his ability to construct preferred teacher identities. Specifically, Jay highlighted how students, especially Josue, resisted his "presence" or position of authority by "derailing" the academic conversation to off-topic laughter. At the end of his reflection, he stated that he wanted to handle those kinds of episodes better and realized that if he could do that, he might be able to situate himself and students in a student-centered classroom. This kind of reflective thinking is different than typical video analysis projects (Sherin & van Es, 2009), because it challenged Jay to examine a specific interaction and write about how his language and behavior reflected his desired identities. From this, Jay learned that teaching is about more than content or a set of strategies. Pedagogy is also about the ability to negotiate positions of power in ways that provide compromise for students and teacher within a classroom. If a teacher struggles to do that, they will have difficulty sharing content and strategies with students.

At the same time, it is evident that Jay needed more support from his teacher education program to help him understand the power structures that existed and how to develop solutions. For Jay, this relates to the dilemma of enacting critical pedagogy practices during his student teaching. We could offer support by providing successful case studies about how teachers negotiate positions of power in ways that allow them to enact their preferred teacher identities. In Chapter Six, we explore such critical conversations in our seminar course.

Throughout this project, we asked ourselves how much analysis could we expect from student teachers? Obviously Jay, an inexperienced teacher, was trying to figure out how to survive and become a better teacher. Is it "too much" to ask him to analyze how his identities shape learning and instruction? If so, is there a place for this kind of identity work in a teacher education program? At the beginning of this piece, we quoted one of Jay's students, whose comment helped us answer this question. In other words, if Jay, and other preservice teachers like him, wish to "level the field," then we must help them develop the necessary tools so that if "they got [him] cussin' . . . [he would come to] know it." Thus, we believe that despite the difficulty, this kind of video and discourse analysis is significant in teacher education because it opens dialogue about how language is used by teacher and students as a negotiating tool for power-share identities to enhance learning (Boling, 2007; Van Es & Sherin, 2004).

TRY IT OUT: EXPLORING POSITIONS OF POWER

To further illustrate these concepts, let's look at a transcript from Monica's classroom. Monica's teaching philosophy stated that she hoped to "engage the students in discussion, research activities that make learning English interesting, and encourage students to be more inquisitive about the world around them." The following transcript from her lesson took place in a ninth-grade on-level English classroom in a rural school in the Southeast United States. Monica's objective was to review what students gathered from a speech analysis assignment examining both Old Major's speech from *Animal Farm* and Martin Luther King's "I Have A Dream Speech." Here we see her opening the lesson with a review of key rhetorical strategies from both speeches and how they are effective. As you read the transcript, think about the following questions: In what ways did Monica situate herself as a power-share or power-control teacher? How did students position Monica? How did Monica position students? How did these positionings align with her philosophy of being engaging, interesting, and encouraging? Use Tables 3.1 and 3.2 as analysis tools for guidance in thinking about positions of power.

> **Monica:** Alright guys! The bell has rung. Let's quiet down and get started. Alright, so what did you guys find for the speech analysis? Look at number one. It says . . .
> {Monica calls a student's attention to the front}.
> **Monica:** Number one. What phrases do the speeches repeat? Do you have yours? I handed them all back to you.
> **Jessica:** I do.
> **Monica:** What did you get Jessica?
> **Jessica:** For Martin Luther, I put one hundred years later and what's the other one? OM?
> **Monica:** Old Major.
> **Jessica:** I put comrades.
> **Monica:** Comrades. And what effect do you think that has?
> **Jessica:** I said, like, it grabs their attention.

48 Positions of Power

Table 3.1 Analysis Chart for Positions of Power

Evidence from transcript (list transcript lines or describe interaction).	Reflexive power-share positions: How does the teacher situate herself as a power-share teacher?	Interactive power-share positions: How does the teacher situate students in power-share positions? How is she positioned by students?	Reflexive power-control positions: How does the teacher situate herself as a power-control teacher?	Interactive power-control positions: How does the teacher situate students in power-control positions? How is she positioned by students?

Table 3.2 Chart for Discourse Analysis of Power Positions

Discourse patterns	How did the discourse patterns shape reflexive positionings?	How did the discourse patterns shape interactive positionings?
What kind of pronouns did she use?		
Number of lines of teacher talk		
Number of lines of students' talk		
Open-ended questions		
Closed-ended questions		
Types of responses (praises, validations, elaborations, etc.)		

Juzwik et al. (2013)

>   **Monica:** It does. It grabs their attention and this is something we refer to in rhetorical devices as anaphora . . . and that's where a phrase within the speech is repeated over and over again and the effect that it has on the audience is that it, you know, constantly drills that point home. It drives a point home. It grabs their attention. Look at, um, the second part of the question, we went over that. Number two. Where do these two speakers-how-where do these two speakers appeal to the oppressed? What did you guys get for that?

Jessica: In line one.
Monica: Huh? In line one, uh, Martin Luther King or Old Major?
Jessica: I didn't write that down.
Monica: No? Carlos, what did you get for number two?
Carlos: They talk about what they want most.
Monica: Yes, they talk about what they want and this is the message they are sending out to the people—to their audience and they, of course, want to bring about anger in them. They want to show them how they're being treated indifferently and what can be done to make it better—what needs to be done as a whole to make it better. And then, um what feeling does it give to the listener?
Jessica: Inspiration.
Monica: Inspiration and they use anger to get that inspiration. Um, what are some key theme words that are repeated over and over in these speeches? Not phrases, but the theme words and Jessica you mentioned one earlier.
Jessica: Comrades?
Monica: Comrades.
Nancy: Freedom.
Monica: Huh?
Nancy: Freedom.
Monica: Freedom, both have freedom, comrades. Why do you think that Old Major is constantly saying comrades over and over and over again?
Jessica: It gets their attention.
Monica: It gets their attention, but also, what does comrades mean?
Carlos: The same side.
Monica: Yes, it's unity. He's trying to tell them, you know, let's get together, you know, we can take over Mr. Jones and we can have all of this stuff for ourselves. So he needs to get them to unify and one means to do that is to let them know they are brothers in arms against one person.

Based on this transcript, we discuss our thoughts on how Monica used language to position herself and her students. For the following discussion, we take note of how students either take up or resist those positionings and what those positionings did for Monica's goals as a teacher.

Overall, it is clear that Monica does most of the talking even though her goal is to promote a discussion about *Animal Farm* with the students. She posed open-ended questions that were answered by the students on paper and handed back to them. Oftentimes giving students the questions prior to the discussion can promote richer conversations because it provides students more time to prepare for the conversation. In this case, however, Monica had a difficult time engaging students right away, as illustrated at the beginning of the excerpt. To promote student talk, she asked for volunteers and then reminded them that they could refer to the discussion sheet that they were just handed. After Jessica shared her answer, Monica repeated what Jessica said. This can be a helpful conversational move for teachers to ensure that the entire class hears a student's response. Monica then asked Jessica a follow-up question about her opinion. After being interrupted by a student, Jessica gave a short response. Monica then elaborated about specific rhetorical devices that relate to grabbing the reader's attention. The same sort of pattern occurred with the next topic exchange. Monica even called on a student, Carlos, in an attempt to foster more participation from the students. Overall, Monica used open-ended questions to engage students in conversation. Students, however, appeared to resist that position by declining to volunteer and expand on discussion questions. As a result, Monica's talk increased and she was positioned as the expert in this conversation. Similar to Jay, then, Monica attempted to enact a power-share identity, but students resisted that position through silence.

How does Monica leverage these concepts to make sense of her classroom interactions? Although the transcript provides some insight into issues of power and status in this classroom, Monica's reflection provides important context for a more constructive interpretation. Thus, we begin with Monica's response to the kinds of questions she posed in her transcript:

> We were working on *Animal Farm* and my questions mainly dealt with reading comprehension. I asked a few analytical questions but I felt defeated in doing so from past experiences with them. I felt like this class in particular wanted me to spoon feed everything to them because every time I asked them an extended engagement question, I would just get shrugs and blanks stares. I did split them into pairs and give them extended engagement questions when we were reading Macbeth and they did well with it. However, I had some students who would just get their partner to answer it for them.

From Monica's analysis, we understand that she is frustrated by her students' lack of participation. Specifically, she described her attempts to foster discussion with extended engagement questions, but she did not receive the participation she hoped for. We recognize, however, that she missed a few opportunities to focus on the assets, rather than deficits (i.e., need to be spoon fed; students just get partners to answer for them) of her students. Through her descriptions of students, she situated herself as powerless to foster discussion in her classroom. As teacher educators, we needed to do a better job of helping preservice teachers who experience frustrations like these to draw from students' assets in order to promote participation and develop a classroom community.

She continued positioning herself as powerless in her response to how she positioned her students as readers and writers; she said:

> I asked them to read aloud and picked students randomly on one occasion. When I go to the second student, he just flat out refused to read it. He apologized to me after school and said he was not a strong reader. I had them read it to themselves but they still complained about it. The point of the story is that I feel I position them as incapable of reading and writing by reading the literature to them and letting them listen to it on CD. When I tell them I will read it to them, I am positioning them as incapable, but I don't know how to accomplish it. I can't force them to read.

In this excerpt, Monica stated that she positioned students as incapable of reading by reading aloud to them in class. Again, she situated herself as powerless by stating that she is unsure about how to situate students as readers when they appear to refuse that position. In addition, her assumptions about what it meant to "be" a reader (listening is not considered reading) shaped how she positioned her students. As literacy educators, we noticed that Monica needed more pedagogical content knowledge about the teaching of reading to students. This is evident when she is unable to provide concrete steps about how to improve her practices. This is typical of novice high school English teachers who learn how to teach literature as opposed to reading. More work in our teacher education program needs to focus on teaching reading to older, struggling students.

Next, she attempted to explain why she is having a hard time thinking about how to provide instruction to fit the needs of her students.

> Students positioned me as a dictator. I did not make my lesson plan fun. I'm not sure how to make this literature fun and this is something I need to work on. When I went to school the transmission model was used. In kindergarten we chanted, "Ma, Me, Mi, Mo, Mu" as the teacher pointed to a poster on the board. In high school, we were given X amount of chapters to read and took a quiz the next day. This is probably why I have a hard time thinking outside the box. We never had fun. It was work, after all. I think this hinders my ability to incorporate engaging activities into my lesson plans because, in the back of my head, I'm thinking this is work, kids—suck it up!

This reflective statement is significant because it illuminated Monica's beliefs about how students should learn. Because she learned in a more skill-and-drill environment, she did not see the purpose in making lessons student-centered or "fun," even though that appeared to be what her students needed. Her acknowledgement of this dilemma, however, illustrates awareness about the different learning preferences between her and her students.

These comments also illustrate how her past teachers shaped her current teacher identities. Because she is receiving different instructional strategies from her university, Monica is having a difficult time negotiating how she learned with expectations from her university and preferences from her students.

Finally, to provide more insight into why Monica has difficulty relating to her students, she admitted that she carries specific prejudices that shape how she positions herself and her students. Below is Monica's response to the question about the ways in which her gender, class, race, and sexuality shape her teaching.

> This [issues of sexual orientation] affects me greatly. I try to hide my opinions. I hope the students cannot read it in my body language and spoken thoughts. I did make a few sexist comments against the boys. Trying to hide my religion is hard for me as well. I get irritated when students make jokes about the strong belief in God during the Middle Ages. I just try to hide my beliefs and be a neutral party in my speech. . . . I need to develop a good rapport with students. I didn't accomplish this in my current teaching practices.

Here, Monica reflected on her ability to remain neutral about issues of sexual orientation, gender, and religion. She hoped that her discomfort or irritability about either matter does not show through in her talk with students. She noted, however, that she already made a few sexist comments against males in her classroom. Such use of language certainly works against the enactment of a power-share identity. After reading Monica's transcript and reflection along with Jay's analysis, what are your thoughts on how Monica might use language in ways that enact a power-share identity in her classroom? How might a power-share identity help or constrain Monica from her goals of engaging "students in discussion, research activities that make learning English interesting, and encouraging students to be more inquisitive about the world around them?"

REFERENCES

Agee, J. (2004). Negotiating a teacher identity: An African American teacher's struggle to teach in test driven contexts. *Teachers College Record, 106*(4), 747–774.

Alsup, J. (2006). *Teacher identity discourses: Negotiating personal and professional spaces*. Mahwah, NJ: Lawrence Erlbaum.

Assaf, L. (2005). Exploring identities in a reading specialization program. *Journal of Literacy Research, 37*(2), 201–236.

Boling, E. (2007). "Yeah, but I still don't want to deal with it." Changes in a teacher candidate's conceptions of inclusion. *Teaching Education, 18*(3), 217–231.

Brooke, R. (1987). Underlife and writing instruction. *College Composition and Communication, 38*, 141–152.

Buzzelli, C., & Johnston, B. (2001). Authority, power, and morality in classroom discourse. *Teaching and Teacher Education, 17*, 873–884.

Cummins, J. (2009). Pedagogies of choice: Challenging coercive relations of power in classrooms and communities. *International Journal of Bilingual Education and Bilingualism, 12*(3), 261–271.
Davies, B., & Harré, R. (1990). Positionings: The discursive production of selves. In B. Davies (Ed.), *A body of writing* (pp. 87–106). New York: AltaMira Press.
Foucault, M. (1979). *Discipline and punish: The birth of the prison*. New York, NY: Vintage.
Freire, P. (2000). *Pedagogy of the oppressed* (30th ed.). New York, NY: Continuum International Publishing Group.
Giroux, H. (2000). *Stealing innocence: Corporate culture's war on children*. New York, NY: Palgrave.
Gutierrez, K., Rymes, B., & Larson, J. (1995). Script, counterscript and underlife in the classroom: James Brown versus Brown v. The Board of Education. *Harvard Educational Review, 65*(3), 445–471.
Handsfield, L. J., Crumpler, T. P., & Dean, T. R. (2010). Tactical negotiations and creative adaptations: The discursive production of literacy curriculum and teacher identities across space-times. *Reading Research Quarterly, 45*(4), 405–431.
Jackson, A. Y. (2001). Multiple Annies: Feminist poststructural theory and the making of a teacher. *Journal of Teacher Education, 52*(5), 386–397.
Juzwik, M. (2006). Performing curriculum: Building ethos through narratives in pedagogical discourse. *Teachers College Record, 108*(4), 489–528.
Kellner, D. (2000). Multiple literacies and critical pedagogies. In P. P. Trifonas (Ed.), *Revolutionary pedagogies—Cultural politics, instituting education, and the discourse of theory* (pp. 362–408). New York, NY: Routledge.
Larson, J., & Irvine, P. (1999). "We call him Dr. King": Reciprocal distancing in urban classrooms. *Language Arts, 65*(5), 393–400.
Linehan, C., & McCarthy, J. (2000). Positioning in practice: Understanding participation in the social world. *Journal for the Theory of Social Behaviour, 30*, 435–453.
Mosley, M. (2010). Becoming a literacy teacher: Approximations in critical literacy teaching. *Teaching Education, 21*(4), 403–426.
Puvirajah, A., Verma, G., & Webb, H. (2012). Examining the mediation of power in a collaborative community: Engaging in informal science as authentic practice. *Cultural Studies of Science Education, 7*, 375–408.
Rex, L., & Schiller, L. (2009). *Using discourse analysis to improve classroom interaction*. New York, NY: Routledge.
Ritchie, S., Rigano, D., & Lowry, J. (2000). Shifting power relations in the "getting of wisdom." *Teaching and Teacher Education, 16*, 165–177.
Rogers, T., Marshall, E., & Tyson, C. A. (2006). Dialogic narratives of literacy, teaching, and schooling: Preparing literacy teachers for diverse settings. *Reading Research Quarterly, 41*(2), 202–224. doi:10.1598/RRQ.41.2.3
Sherin, M. G., & van Es, E. (2009). Effects of video club participation on teacher's professional vision. *Journal of Teacher Education, 60*(1), 20–37.
Smagorinsky, P., Cook, L. S., Moore, C., Jackson, A. Y., & Fry, P. G. (2004). Tensions in learning to teach: Accommodation and the development of a teaching identity. *Journal of Teacher Education, 55*(1), 8–24.
van Es, E., & Sherin, M. G. (2002). Learning to notice: Scaffolding new teachers interpretations of classroom interactions. *Journal of Technology and Teacher Education, 10*(4), 571–596.
Watson, C. (2006): Narratives of practice and the construction of identity in teaching. *Teachers and Teaching: Theory and Practice, 12*(5), 509–526.

4   Positions of Advocacy

In this chapter, we explore how one preservice teacher examined positions of advocacy during her time as a student teacher. To begin, we provide a brief scenario. In a written reflection about an observed classroom interaction, Erica (a preservice teacher in a high school English classroom) reflected on the behavior of a young man. In her description, she explained he had "spotty attendance" because he had "a lot going on in his life." During an observation with her cooperating teacher, this student put his head down on the desk. Erica elaborated:

> I asked him if he was paying attention, and he said no. I asked him if he was still focused on succeeding, something that he and I have discussed. He said yes, but then shut his book and folder and put his arm out with his head on it. . . . My supervisor, after his observation, criticized my handling of the situation, saying that sitting down one-on-one with him and asking him to complete a small portion of the work would have been a better approach. . . . The next day . . . I asked him (along with the whole class) how they thought I performed during my observation. They said I seemed nervous, but the student who put his head down said I did a good job. . . . He apologized for his behavior and said that he thought about what I asked him about success and though he was a little embarrassed, needed a reality check. He was on point the entire rest of the week.

During the student teaching experience, Erica identified her desire to be a teacher who is a caring advocate for her students. In this reflection, she expressed her difficulty with enacting this identity because of several constraints. First, she has difficulty involving a student who is disengaged because of "spotty" attendance. Second, in an effort to enact a caring identity, she risked embarrassing the student by putting him on the spot. She questioned her interactions based on her supervisor's response that she should have handled the situation differently. To further complicate the situation, her student gave her different input on the interaction in a discussion the following day and indicated that her response motivated him to participate more in class that week. At the end of the reflection, she continued to reflect about the "best" way to respond to the student during this interaction in ways that enabled her to enact her preferred teacher identities. Although she did not resolve her dilemma, we believe that this kind of thoughtful reflection about classroom interactions can help candidates take up desired teacher identities. We begin with this excerpt to illustrate the complex ways that preservice teachers struggle to construct and enact preferred teaching identities related to advocacy, especially those associated with social equity teaching (Alsup, 2006; Haniford, 2010; Lazar, Edwards, & McMillon, 2012; Smagorinsky, Cook, Moore, Jackson, & Fry, 2004).

SOCIAL EQUITY TEACHING

Research illustrates differences in the school experiences of culturally and linguistically diverse students in the United States (Darling-Hammond, 2010; Sleeter, 2008). For instance, nearly half of our nation's African American students, nearly 40% of Latino students, and only 11% of White students attend high schools in which graduation is not the norm (Balfanz & Letgers, 2004). In addition, absentee rates in high school range from 6 percent to 23 percent, with high poverty urban areas reporting up to one-third of students chronically absent. In poor rural areas, one in four students miss at least a month's worth of school (Balfanz & Byrnes, 2012). Being aware of these statistics as an educator is important for understanding how to meet the needs of current students. Much work, however, must be done to develop dispositions needed to foster the success of culturally and linguistically diverse students. Specifically, educational researchers have encouraged teacher education and professional development that focuses on recognition of a "child's literate potential," utilization of "students' culture to inform teaching" (Lazar et al., 2012, p. 2), and development of an advocacy stance (Cochran-Smith, 2004). This can be difficult when teachers come from different cultural and linguistic backgrounds than their students. Specifically, research suggests that White teachers do not always understand the school experiences of underprivileged students and struggle to see and foster the literate potential of such students (Sleeter, 2008). In particular, White preservice teachers avoid discussions of race and racism for fear of saying the wrong thing or sounding racist (Levine-Rasky, 2000; McIntyre, 1997). According to Villegas & Irvine (2010), teachers of color are more likely to understand the experiences and potential of their students, but struggle to use that knowledge to develop curriculum and strategies that build on that potential. Specifically, culturally responsive teaching has not been integrated thoroughly and consistently in teacher education programs. As a result, many teacher candidates report feeling underprepared to teach culturally and linguistically diverse students (Kea, Trent, & Davis, 2002). In addition, all teachers struggle to negotiate the demands of skill-and-drill practice promoted for achievement on high-stakes standardized exams with instruction designed to fit the needs of individual students and classroom cultures (Darling-Hammond, 2010).

To address these issues, educational research has investigated aspects of social equity teaching (Lazar et al., 2012), such as culturally responsive teaching (Gay, 2000). Social equity teaching recognizes that students learn within social, political, and cultural contexts and advocates for students by focusing on the assets of students' literacy capabilities in ways that attempt to offset social inequalities. Such instruction fosters culturally relevant and intellectually rich classroom communities. Teachers who practice social equity instruction consistently evaluate their own cultural positions and knowledge in ways that shape instructional practices based on the needs of students. In *Bridging Literacy and Equity*, Lazar et al. (2012) describe the following six dimensions of social equity teaching within literacy classrooms: (a) societal factors that influence literacy achievement; (b) complexity and significance of culture; (c) culturally situated nature of literacy and language; (d) third space; (e) literacy instruction as a critical and socially transformative practice; and (e) personal transformation toward action. We describe each of those dimensions below.

Societal factors that influence literacy achievement include historical, political, cultural, and economic factors, such as poverty or racism. To explore such issues, teacher educators might foster an examination of how poverty impacts individual learning and explore the social capital that exists in the communities of non-dominant groups. By studying the relationship between societal factors and literacy achievement, teacher educators can better identify their own responsibility for positively affecting students' life trajectories.

A second dimension of social equity teaching includes investigating the complexity and significance of culture. In this dimension, teacher candidates examine how "culture is multifaceted, socially constructed, learned, dynamic, and shaped by power" (Lazar et al., 2012, p. 14). Through this area of study, future teachers learn how to move beyond the "Heroes and Holidays" approach to curriculum design toward the daily integration of pedagogical moves, such as facilitating meaningful conversation about multicultural literature or developing relationships with students and caregivers.

A third dimension examines the culturally situated nature of language and literacy, by questioning normative or accepted literacy practices. Thus, preservice teachers might challenge how the languages and literacies of non-dominant groups do or do not align with those of the mainstream. Future teachers, then, are better prepared to recognize the legitimacy of all languages and literacies and teach from an asset-focused approach.

Fourth, social equity focuses on third space teaching, a concept that sustains students' culture in the curriculum by building on "students' literary and linguistic knowledge and community resources to either build bridges between local knowledge traditions and school knowledge or to create and transform school knowledge" (Lazar et al., 2012, p. 15). This can be done by drawing from everyday funds of knowledge (Gonzalez, Moll, & Amanti, 2013) or drawing on specific discourse patterns of students to foster opportunities for learning.

A fifth dimension suggests the importance of treating literacy instruction as a transformative practice. In other words, teachers create and use curriculum that challenges and recognizes oppressive systems. This includes project-based instruction and learning that expects students to promote change related to social justice issues in their communities.

Lazar et al. (2012) argue that teachers who practice strong literacy instruction and social equity teaching are better situated to challenge schools that do not benefit students. In particular, teachers are able to negotiate between the demands of the institution (e.g., high-stakes exams, scripted curriculum) in ways that provide meaningful instruction. The authors describe strong literacy instruction as practices that include creating a literacy rich environment, explicit literacy instruction, a focus on individual needs, development of strong connections with students and caregivers, and weaving in of reading, writing, and content area themes.

Because social equity teaching is cultivated over time, preservice teachers would benefit from teacher education programs that foster systematic opportunities for preservice teachers to enact and examine teacher identities related to the aforementioned dimensions of literacy and social equity. One desired identity we focus on in this chapter involves enacting an advocate identity for students. To examine that identity work, we focus on the following questions:

- In what ways did one preservice teacher engage in identity work related to advocacy through the discourse analysis of video-recorded lessons?
- What micro- and macro-level supports and constraints (e.g., language choices and school policies) shaped that identity work?

ERICA'S DESIRED TEACHING IDENTITIES: ADVOCATE

Erica, a European American female in her early twenties, was enrolled in a master's level English education program in a large public university in the northeast United States. She was required to complete 60 days of student teaching at Clinton High School (CHS) (pseudonym), which is a small secondary school in a large urban city. A majority of the student body at CHS is African American and Latino/a. High school students that attend this school have had difficulties both socially and academically in previous high schools, and attend CHS to complete credit requirements to graduate and pass state exams.

Erica's philosophy of herself as a teacher reflected a desire to position herself as an advocate for her students. In her teaching philosophy, she explained: "As a teacher, my philosophy is to educate a whole person, one who has a past and a future, as well as who is presently in my classroom . . . [through] attention to learning for both my students and for myself." Thus, she positioned her students as multidimensional and characterized her teaching as attending to her students' previous life experiences and future goals. In keeping with Lazar et al.'s (2012) framework, Erica demonstrates an understanding that there are multiple factors that influence student learning. She also signifies teaching as a simultaneous learning experience and acknowledges the roles her students play in helping her learn more about herself and her practice—a disposition needed for transforming her practices to relate to her students' needs and the classroom context.

As Erica came to know her students at CHS, she positioned her students as struggling in their personal lives in ways that she had not experienced. Throughout Erica's seminar course, teacher candidates posted weekly about their student teaching experiences to a course website discussion forum. Using the discussion forum, Erica contemplated how to support her students through curriculum to address issues of gang violence, poverty, and depression. Early in the semester, she wrote: "Working in the [city] public schools brings a unique challenge for me, I've found. Almost all (with the exception of one, maybe two) of my students have HARD lives" (emphasis original). Melissa also interviewed Erica after the course was completed to find out more about her student teaching experience and the impact of course assignments on developing her teacher identities. During the interview, Erica recounted:

> A lot of the students I worked with had a lot of trouble with the law, or drugs or gangs, or things like that, so, I mean that's a lot of baggage for someone who is 16 or 17 years old. I think it's impossible not to consider that when you're teaching . . . as someone who's from a different educational background . . . I didn't consider how much you have to consider the person at first, so once I realized that I was instantly more successful at teaching.

Consistent with her philosophy, Erica considered her students' lives and this informed how she positioned herself in the classroom as an advocate for her students' social and academic needs. To enact this identity, she shared that she made thoughtful choices about curriculum and built caring relationships with students to attend to the multiple dimensions of their lives. In the classroom, she positioned her teaching as engaging students to use writing and literacy to process hardships they experience outside of school. This stance toward curriculum also aligns with Lazar et al.'s (2012) dimension of social equity teaching related to engaging literacy instruction as a transformational practice. Early in the semester she posted to the discussion forum: "I teach a Freedom Writer's class and we specifically discuss and write about these difficulties, which I think is a positive outlet [for students]." Thus,

Erica's posts demonstrate that part of her desired teaching identities is to be a caring advocate who bridges her students' literacy learning with their social and emotional well being.

Lastly, Erica's personal identities reflected her teacher identities. In a teaching portfolio she created as part of her MA culminating project, she described herself as "a wife, daughter, sister and soon to be a mother" and stated that these personal identities "contribute to my teaching, because just as a student is a whole person, so is a teacher." Consistent with an advocate stance, Erica wrote about how she went back to school for education to answer a calling she had felt for many years whilst pursuing a career as a writer. She explained that "teaching [urban] kids made the calling even stronger" and that she looked forward to the ability to "improve the education of the next generation" of children in the city where she had decided to raise her own family. From this description, we see Erica translate and negotiate (Alsup, 2006) her personal familial identities with her professional identities as a teacher and advocate for students whom she feels have been underserved by the city's school system.

We understand that as a White, middle class female some of Erica's desires may be open to criticism for demonstrating a savior mentality with youth of color who live in underprivileged circumstances. However, we attend to what her statements reveal about her desired teaching identities as related to Lazar et al.'s framework. Because Erica desired to put her students' needs above her own and to learn from her students, we frame her desired teaching identities as a caring advocate rather than a savior. Erica's stance and identity enactments offer a model for how a White, middle class teacher may enact identities related to equity, which was a noted concern among our teacher candidates whose personal identities reflected race and class privilege. Next, we turn to how Erica both enacted and struggled to enact her desired teaching identities related to advocacy in the classroom.

POSITIONS OF ADVOCACY

To explore Erica's positions of advocacy, we first discuss how she investigated how her enactments aligned with her desired teacher identities through discourse analysis. To end, we explain how Erica examined the ways in which her enactments misaligned with desired teacher identities through discourse analysis. In both sections, we describe how Erica analyzed the ways in which personal and institutional micro- and macro-level supports and constraints impacted those alignments and misalignments.

Enacting an Advocate Identity by Establishing Classroom Culture

In all three of the assignments, Erica identified moments when she successfully aligned aspects of her practice with her desired teaching identities through her nonverbal behaviors and language choices. For instance, her classroom setup was configured in a small circle of desks rather than rows and she spoke to students in a consistently respectful manner. She also maintained a calm, even tone and teacher presence and addressed her students as adults who were capable of making their own decisions. Erica noticed this aspect of her practice in her reflection of her first video; she described how she established a relaxed classroom environment for learning by creating a welcoming atmosphere:

> In this class, and all of the time, I speak to the students in a friendly, conversational tone. I enjoy talking with them and teaching them and I try to make that clear in my tone of voice . . . so I feel as though my tone is authentic and successful toward the end of creating a comfortable classroom.

In this excerpt, Erica engages in analysis about how her tone positions herself as approachable ("friendly, conversational") and her students as valued contributors (someone she enjoys talking to). In addition, her statement that she explicitly attempts to use her tone of voice to illustrate her desire to talk to students aligns with her desired identities to be a caring advocate for student-centered talk. Erica's analysis is significant because she is aware that her tone, not just the content of her talk, has the power to position her in particular ways that shape how she is perceived by students and how she enacts her desired teacher identities. In addition, she acknowledges that her tone also impacts the classroom community ("comfortable"), which could shape how students engage in learning and see her as a teacher who has their best interests in mind. Her last statement notes that she attempts to listen to students' questions and wants to ensure that they understand what is being taught. Such practices are related to dimensions of social equity teaching that encourage the development of a third space, specifically building on the discourse patterns of students (Lazar et al., 2012).

Enacting an Advocate Identity through Transformative Curriculum

To further explore how Erica examined her desired identities in practice, we present an extended vignette from her first teaching video and reflection assignment. For the lesson, Erica's goal was to review a non-fiction reading previously covered on political conflict and genocide in Sudan. She then wanted students to compare this reading with a poem written by a former student. The poem detailed the hardships the author faced related to violence and poverty. The purpose of this lesson was to prepare students to use both texts to write comparatively on the theme of struggle as practice for their upcoming state language arts exam. These curricular choices were consistent with Erica's desire to use curriculum to help students process difficulties they faced in their lives and Lazar et al.'s dimension for bridging literacy and equity teaching through transformative practice.

During the lesson, a student (Jamal) expresses his need to reread the materials. He begins by asking Erica if he needs to read both "Too Many Evils" and the poem written by the student. Erica responds to his question:

> Jamal: We're gonna use "Too Many Evils Darken the Sky" and this poem?
> Erica: Yep, I'll write it on the board. We read that, and if you need to re-read it . . .
> Jamal: We read this right?
> Erica: We read that, and if you need to re-read it . . .
> Jamal: Yeah, I'll read it . . .
> Erica: If you need to re-read you should have plenty of time to read and to write, uh, the paragraph in the period so try to finish by the end of the period.
> Jamal: We gotta read both of them right?
> Erica: Yeah.
> Jamal: Yeah, I need to re-read 'em.

In her reflection about the above interaction, Erica acknowledged how her micro-level language choices positioned the student as a capable reader who is able to make his own choices to guide comprehension of the material:

> I also try to individually answer questions, for example when the student asked if we already read 'Too Many Evils . . .' I respond, "We read that, and if you need to re-read it . . .' I think it is good that I did not issue a directive, such as "Reread it," even though I knew he needed to. Like most people, J. likes to make his own decisions.

Erica engaged in discourse analysis that highlights how she attempted to enact an advocate position for his literacy learning. In particular, she provided an example from the interaction that illustrates how she intentionally did not issue a directive and provided space for Jamal to make his own decisions as a reader. Specifically, Erica reimagined how different language choices (i.e., directives) might have impacted her relationship with her student and how he positioned himself as a learner. Rather than tell him what she knew he needed to do, Erica noticed that she carefully negotiates the classroom interaction to guide the student in applying a strategy to support his comprehension. Thus, her own discourse analysis of this event allows Erica to capture and articulate how word choices became conscious elements of advocacy in the classroom (Juzwik, 2006), supporting her preferred teacher identities.

In the next example, Erica reflected about how her language choices with her student (Alton) and cooperating teacher (Bob) shaped her enactment as an advocate. We provide the interaction first and the reflection second.

> **Alton:** Can I have a dictionary?
> **Bob:** No dictionaries.
> **Alton:** We can't?
> **Erica:** You wouldn't have one on the [state exam].
> **Alton:** I don't know what a word means.
> **Bob:** Well, all right, [Erica], if you want to let them use it that's your call.
> **Alton:** I mean, it's for my own benefit. I just don't know the word . . .
> **Bob:** But it's not a true assessment if you have help.
> **Alton:** Well, I guess I won't know the word.
> **Bob:** Do you agree Erica . . . or do you want to let him do it?
> **Erica:** I disagree . . . because I think it's an assessment . . .
> **Bob:** Go ahead.
> **Erica:** . . . but an exercise as well.
> **Alton:** It doesn't make any sense.
> **Erica:** Well I rather that he know it so that if he wants to use it on the actual exam . . .

In Erica's analysis of the event, she recognized how she enacts her preferred teacher identities as an advocate for students despite the resistance from her cooperating teacher:

> In this situation, we [Erica & Bob] agree through body language to have the disagreement in front of the students. As I suspected and later confirmed with him, it was a bit of a good cop/bad cop role. He initially didn't want [Alton] to use the dictionary, but stuck with that line of thinking in order for the students to see my line of reason for defending them. I explain that I think this assignment is "an assessment but an exercise as well." Further, I explain that I'd rather he learn the word and have it in his vocabulary for future use. . . . The students went on to write their paragraphs after these discussions, and after class Alton approached me and said that he appreciated my advocacy and felt that my gentler hand in the classroom was enabling his learning. . . . I think that my advocacy of Alton supports him as a student and as a reader and writer.

From her analysis, Erica acknowledged that Bob positioned her as a teacher capable of making informed decisions about teaching and learning. In addition, she stated that she and her cooperating teacher situated each other as "good cop/bad cop" to allow her to build rapport with students and ultimately enact the advocate identities that she preferred. Specifically, she mentioned her word choice of "assessment but an exercise as well" to illustrate how she attempted to make the assignment purposeful for her students while also satisfying her cooperating teacher. In other words, she purposefully chose those words during her teaching to try and negotiate conflicting positions. She noticed, then, that her teacher identities are impacted not only by how students position her but also by how colleagues position her through verbal and nonverbal exchanges. Furthermore, Erica noted that Alton positioned her as an advocate ("appreciated my advocacy") through humorous exchanges, which solidified how she successfully enacted her preferred teacher identities. This kind of feedback from students is important for Erica because it confirms that students are interpreting interactions in the ways she intended. Finally, Erica acknowledges that she positioned her student as a reader and writer who can use tools (the dictionary) to support his reading and writing skills, beyond the test. Those reflective statements represent Erica's ideas that learning is more than merely assessment. As stated, this belief bumped up against the ideology of her cooperating teacher. Fortunately, Erica was able to negotiate that tension with the support of Bob and her students. This validation is important because it can guide her future behavior. Overall, Erica recognized how she used verbal and nonverbal language to navigate the conflicting beliefs between students and colleagues in ways that allowed her to position herself as an advocate.

Moments of Struggle in Enacting an Advocate Identity

Erica also used discourse analysis to examine moments when she was unable to enact her preferred teacher identities. In addition, she noted how macro-level power structures challenged her ability to fully enact her desired teaching identities. As stated, we know Erica desired to be a teacher who facilitates student learning and listens to her students to inform her pedagogical decisions. This was not always easy for Erica to manage, especially as a student teacher in a school under pressure to improve student performance on high-stakes exams. Erica noted that in the following interaction related to the student-authored poem mentioned earlier in the chapter, she missed an important opportunity to talk about the meaning and relevance of the poem to students' lives.

[Erica distributes the poem and students begin to read it silently.]

>**Alton:** Some people really have it bad.
>**Erica:** That's right. It's really well-written. It's really nice. Poem of my life. And then we're going to use "Evils." And then our controlling idea is struggle. Does anyone have any questions?

In particular, Erica wrote that she struggled to figure out how to react to Alton's comment in response to the student-authored poem. Although the poet's name was kept anonymous, the poem presented personal hardships that connected with the class theme of struggle. Students were very curious about the author of this poem, and asked Erica whether the poet was a male or female and if the author's school schedule was similar to their own. Erica explains that she chose the text because it connected to the lives of students and potentially garnered interest from them. Under pressure to prepare students for the test, however, Erica reflects on how she missed an opportunity to critically discuss the student-authored poem with her students. Erica, feeling compelled to move students into writing about the controlling idea of struggle, responded briefly in agreement that the poem is "well-written" and pushed the group to continue to focus on their writing for the assessment. Reviewing her video and transcripts, Erica notices how the student personally responded to the poem and how her response contradicted with how she viewed herself as a teacher:

> That was an opportunity for a discussion on so many different topics; education being just one. Sometimes, it is important to stay on task in a 45 min. class and that was my focus at that time. I probably won't do it different for that reason, but in an ideal situation, I would engage the class in a discussion about how some people do have it bad and how we can help them and ourselves.

In this reflection, Erica notes that she positions herself as a teacher more concerned with staying on task than engaging in a relevant discussion with students, a misalignment with her preferred identities to advocate for equity and her students' needs through curriculum in transformative ways. Specifically, she states that she missed an opportunity to facilitate student-led conversation by choosing specific types of talk over others, such as teacher-driven talk versus student-centered dialogue. Thus, Erica was aware that her word choice shaped the direction of the conversation and had potential to shut down some student talk. Whereas Erica reflected on the need for more critical dialogue with students, she also retracts this by saying that kind of dialogue is only possible within an "ideal" classroom situation. Thus, Erica struggles to situate herself through her preferred teaching identities in this example. Erica's interpretation of school-based pressures to prepare students for the state-level exam at the macro-level impacted her ability to enact her desired teaching identities as an advocate. She is aware of how pressure to cover content complicated and ultimately trumped her desire to allow students' interests and needs to guide discussion. Although her awareness of these institutional issues is important, she does not discuss how she might prepare students to succeed on high-stakes exams while also facilitating student-led discussion. Thus, she appears to believe an advocate cannot help students succeed on high-stakes exams. Overall, through discourse analysis, Erica recognized how she used her language to shut down dialogue for the sake of skill-and-drill practice.

Erica further noted from this classroom interaction, however, that she might rush students too much during discussions. She wrote in her reflection on this classroom event: "I intend on listening more carefully and responding more thoughtfully to the students' responses. Sometimes, I breeze past some good answers . . . when slowing down and examining how the answer might better serve the discussion would be better." Thus, Erica realized her tendency to rush past students' talk to keep the discussion moving—noting that in the moment she thought she was advocating for students' needs, but was in fact controlling the discussion and facilitating test preparation versus student discussion. She noted a misalignment between how she reflexively positioned herself as an advocate that positions students as co-constructors of the discussion, and how the video analysis reveals that she instead positions her students' comments as less valued than she intended. This is a sophisticated reflection that is challenging for novice (and experienced) teachers. Based on examining her teacher philosophy in practice, Erica recognized that in the future she needed to listen more to students to guide the direction and content of classroom dialogue.

Erica's Reflection on the Video Analysis Assignment

Erica reflected on the process of using positioning theory to understand her identity work in her third iteration of the assignment:

> I have a record of how my relationship with my students has grown. It is important to see where you stumble, how you speak, and how your body language speaks to the class. In the first video, I appear stiff, I stumble over my words and I made some missteps in communicating and positioning myself as a teacher. . . . There are definitely always things to be improved upon, but I think continually analyzing your teaching, especially through video, is an excellent tool for self-improvement. Inevitably, the way you think you teach in the moment and the way you teach when looking at it from outside the moment is different. Being able to identify and adjust the disparity is invaluable.

As stated, the project created opportunities for Erica to identify how she made sense of her teaching identities and how they matched with her practice. As Erica reported, she noticed growth across the three videos that she completed over time in regards to how her relationship with her students developed. Specifically, she noticed changes in her nonverbal language (appearing stiff) and how this impacted the classroom environment. She also noted the subtle impact that micro-level language choices (e.g., tone, various word choices) had on her ability to enact her desired teaching identities. Although Erica did not complete a trajectory of her learning throughout all three videos (that was not the assignment), she does notice the value in examining enactments of teaching in order to make purposeful adjustments.

This relates to Olsen, as cited by Sexton (2008), who supports that tracking such learning "reveals a process—a path, of sorts—by which individuals can become more conscious, and in more control, of the contours of their own professional development" (p. 14–15). This statement confirms findings that Erica used discourse analysis to examine how she enacted her desired teacher identities during moment-to-moment classroom interactions. Furthermore, she recognized moments in which these enactments both aligned and misaligned with her preferred teacher identities. When misalignments occurred, Erica observed that macro-level influences (pressure to perform skill-and-drill practice for high-stakes exams) and her own language choices impacted how she envisioned her teaching and what occurred in practice. Thus, discourse analysis was a useful tool for Erica to engage in identity work, especially as it related to positions of advocacy. Perhaps such work could be used to promote social equity teaching with teacher candidates or current teachers in professional development contexts.

Such analysis could also foster opportunities for teacher candidates to discuss how to negotiate an advocate identity with contrasting pressures from administration and the district (e.g., to take on a skill-and-drill teacher identity in the name of test achievement). For example, Erica wrote about a time when she shut down a student comment about a poem they read in order to move on to test practice. She observed that this interactional choice positioned the students as non-participants in the classroom. Thus, through her word choice, she told students that their personal interest in a poem is not valued in the class. What is valued, however, is test practice. Although this conflicted with her preferred goals of advocating for students and integrating relevant material into the curriculum, she recognized that institutional constraints and pressures impact the choices teachers make, opening dialogue about how to negotiate such dilemmas. In particular, in-depth discussions about these specific events could help teachers make interactional shifts that open up new ways of positioning from students (Vetter, Meacham, & Schieble 2013).

Erica's analysis also confirmed that students situated her as an advocate. For instance, she noted that one of her students situated her as an advocate when he thanked her for sticking up for his dictionary use in class. In addition, another student affirmed that her comments about his disengagement changed his behavior. Thus, Erica was able to see that students positioned her in ways that she intended. Identity work is complex. It is a negotiation that depends on the people around us. If we intend to facilitate, but students situate us as lecturers by not engaging in conversation, then we have to reevaluate how we enact that facilitator position. When we are perceived in the way we intend to be perceived, teaching and learning become more fluid and comfortable. When we are perceived in unintended ways, we must figure out the root of the misconnection.

Although Erica's analysis opened opportunities for her to engage in identity work, some opportunities were missed. One area we noted that needed more scrutiny was how her personal identities (e.g., White, female) influenced practice and curricular decisions. Considering the situated context of her identities, her experiences with schooling, and her students' identities, Erica wrote in her third video reflection:

> Though there are some race, class and gender differences between my students and me, I try not to let them dominate the relationship, though I remain respectful of our differences. I think it is important as a teacher to learn from your students, to pay attention to what they are telling you.

Although Erica did not name her race, class, and gender differences as related to a position of privilege working with underprivileged students, she does demonstrate critical reflection on how to equalize the power relationship by learning from her students and using their lives and experiences as a guide for building relationships and facilitating learning. Beyond acknowledging that many of her students experienced hardships in life that differed greatly from her own, Erica struggles to move from making curricular choices about readings (e.g., short stories on genocide in Sudan and a student-authored poem) to facilitating the level of critical dialogue and higher order thinking needed to help students process these readings in relation to their lives, as encouraged by social equity teaching (Lazar et al., 2012). Using discourse analysis to reflect upon these moments can help teacher educators to assist preservice teachers to set goals and strategies for improving their practice in particular areas. Although Erica clearly became more comfortable with this kind of analysis over time by using word choice as evidence of her positions, deeper analysis using language as evidence could improve interactional awareness even more.

TRY IT OUT: EXPLORING POSITIONS OF ADVOCACY

To further illustrate positions of advocacy, let's look at a transcript from Ruby's classroom. Ruby's teaching philosophy stated that she wanted to be a teacher who "inspires and challenges her students to exceed their own expectations of their abilities." This goal was due to a teacher she had that pushed her to do even better than she thought she could do in her high school English classroom. Although Ruby did not identify as an advocate for her students, the goal of pushing students beyond their own expectations is one that both culturally relevant pedagogy and social equity teaching encourage and support as a characteristic of advocacy. Let's take a look at a lesson that Ruby recorded with a group of tenth-grade students. As you read, ask yourself the following questions: In what ways did Ruby advocate for her students during this lesson? Did they situate her as an advocate? What more could she have done? Use Table 4.1 and Table 4.2, below, for guidance.

68 *Positions of Advocacy*

Table 4.1 Analysis Chart for Positions of Advocacy

Evidence from transcript (list transcript lines or describe interaction).	Reflexive Positioning: In what ways did Ruby position herself as an advocate for students?	Interactive Positioning: In what ways did Ruby position her students as capable learners, readers, and writers?	Interactive Positioning: In what ways did students position Ruby as an advocate?

Table 4.2 Chart for Discourse Analysis of Power Positions

Discourse patterns	How did the discourse patterns shape reflexive positionings?	How did the discourse patterns shape interactive positionings?
Open-ended questions		
Closed-ended questions		
Teacher responses (praises, elaborations, extensions, validations, etc.)		
Student responses		

Juzwik et al. (2013)

Ruby, an African American student teacher, taught in a classroom of predominately African American students. To provide context for her lesson, she wrote the following description:

> I chose to record a lesson on fallacies in my Honors English II second block class. In the video, I show parts of my warm-up, which asked students to write down answers to these questions: *Which 3 fallacies do you believe are most represented in the media? In what ways can you prevent using fallacies in your own writing (list at least 4)? If any, which fallacy are you having trouble understanding?* After that, I showed the students 3 cartoons and asked them to guess which fallacy was

Positions of Advocacy 69

represented, and in the video I show bits and pieces of that discussion. Next, we watched two commercials—a Kay Hagan Obamacare commercial and a Dodge Charger commercial—and asked the class which fallacies were represented. At the end of class, I gave the students magazines and asked them to find 3 different advertisements with fallacies in them, and to briefly explain which fallacy is depicted.

 The following transcript illustrated the part of the lesson in which students and teacher watched a commercial created by Americans for Prosperity, titled *Tell Kay Hagan Obamacare Hurts North Carolina*. In this commercial, a middle-aged woman explains that since Obamacare has been implemented, her insurance costs her 20 percent more, a reality that Kay Hagan promised would not happen. After watching the commercial, students talk about the following fallacies:

> Julianna: They don't like her because she's a Democrat.
> Ruby: Well, I like this one because I have personally seen this one a lot. What fallacy is represented in this commercial?
> Everett: Appeal to p . . .
> Ada: It's the personal attack one.
> Ruby: Okay, you could say, I see personal attack too because when people say "Obamacare," that's a personal attack because it's not The Obamacare, it's called The Affordable Care Act. That's what it's actually called. People attach Obama to this because they want to personally attack him.
> Maureen: Shouldn't that be illegal to be on TV?
> Ruby: They're saying, "Kay Hagan hurts North Carolina."
> Julianna: She doesn't hurt NC; she helps NC.
> Ruby: Okay, but that's not what this commercial is saying—this commercial is saying she hurts NC. But the one specific fallacy that I want you guys to think about is. . . . Okay, notice how it's taking Sheila Salter's story, right? She is *one* person and they're saying, Obamacare hurt Sheila Salter and then they're like, okay, Obamacare hurts NC. Okay, wait a minute. So how are they taking this one person—you got it?
> Julianna: I have a question. Did they just randomly choose her and tell her to tell her story about Obama?
> Ruby: Yeah, I don't know. We don't know if she's a paid actress. I would *guess* that she's a paid actress because most of the times the people in these commercials *are*. I mean, I'm guessing so. We don't know if this is actually her situation, we don't even know if this is her real name. So that's how we get these commercials—we don't know. But okay, look at how they're taking Sheila Salter's story and they're saying,

70 *Positions of Advocacy*

"Obamacare hurts NC." So what fallacy is it when you don't have a lot of evidence and you're making—guys, listen—so what fallacy is it when you take one person's story and you kind of attribute it to a whole group of people?

Everett: Appeal to ignorance.

Maureen: Hasty generalization.

Ruby: Yes, hasty generalization. This is hasty generalization too, okay? Sheila Salter is *one* person and to say that because Obamacare hurt Sheila Salter that now Obamacare hurts NC—that's a hasty generalization. It hurt this person and now her insurance is super high.

Ada: What's the difference between hasty generalization and slippery slope because they kind of sound the same?

Ruby: They do kind of sound the same in *this* one because it's like, okay, Obamacare hurts Sheila Salter and then Obamacare hurts NC and you could argue that too, but I think this one is definitely hasty generalization because a hasty generalization can happen, say if I walk into this classroom and I say "oh my god, all [DHS] students are well-behaved" because I saw this one class. Okay, you only saw one class, right? So you can't make that assumption. So we've only seen Sheila Salter's story so how can we make the *assumption* that Obamacare hurts every person in NC.

In this transcript, Ruby enacted an advocate identity in two ways. First, Ruby's objective of the lesson is to teach students how to question commonplace assumptions about political ad campaigns. Rather than take Sheila's story at face value, Ruby taught students how to deconstruct what they were viewing through the understanding of fallacies. In particular, she used an ad that was played repetitively at this particular time, so students most likely had seen it. In addition, this kind of analysis supported the kind of literacy that will help students become informed voters and citizens.

Ruby also positioned herself as an advocate through her responses to students' comments and questions. The majority of her responses validated student remarks and then challenged them to think beyond their initial response. For example, in the last response, Ruby agreed with Ada who says that hasty generalization and slippery slope are similar ("They do kind of sound the same"). She then used an example that includes students and their school to help them see the difference. She used a similar approach when Ada answers "personal attack" and Ruby says, " I see personal attack too" and elaborates on her thoughts. We view these validations and elaborations as ways of taking on an advocacy identity associated with social equity teaching because she attempts to validate student perspectives and elaborate with specific examples or ideas that helped them think more about the topic.

We do recognize, however, that Ruby missed a few opportunities by engaging in an Initiate, Respond, and Evaluate (IRE) pattern. What might have happened if Ruby asked others what they thought before she elaborated or asked more questions? How might those kinds of questions positioned students? How might that discourse pattern help her to take on an advocacy position?

Ruby also situated herself as an advocate in her analysis. Below, take note of how she positioned her students.

> My students posed really interesting questions and our discussion lasted quite a bit longer than what shows up in the video. I posed open-ended, leading questions where I tried to get the students to come to the conclusion for themselves rather than me telling them all of the "right" answers. When I asked, "Which fallacy is represented in the comic/commercial?" I wanted to facilitate a discussion about which answers could be a possibility and work through them together as a class. The majority of answers that were thrown out were right on track; my students even thought about answers I didn't even think were possibilities in a way that made a lot of sense to me.

From this analysis, it is clear that Ruby situated her students as valuable participants who pose "really interesting questions" and share "answers I didn't even think were possibilities." From these descriptive phrases of her students, it is clear that Ruby wanted to facilitate conversation to promote dialogue as opposed to assessing for answers that she wants to hear. By doing this, she built on the assets of her students (what they know), rather than their deficits (what they don't know). Students left class knowing more about persuasive language.

Ruby ended her analysis with this reflective paragraph about how her positionings aligned with her desired teacher identities.

> I was surprised that my practices do match up with the teacher I want to become. I want to be a teacher that questions her students and pushes them to think. I want to be a teacher that praises them when they get it, and praises them when they're almost there. I want to be a guide, a facilitator of student learning, and I wanted to create a community of learners. Though I'm not 100% there, I'm definitely headed in the right direction.

What do you think? Does Ruby create a community of learners? If so, how? What more could she do to facilitate student learning and push them to think even more? Take a look at her analysis chart (Table 4.3) for guidance in answering those questions.

Table 4.3 Ruby's Analysis Chart

Evidence from video	How did you position yourself as a teacher? A guide, a coach	How did students position you as a teacher? A guide, a coach	How did you position your students as readers, writers, and students? Leaders in their own learning
Example one:	I questioned them. When I asked them which fallacy was represented in the comics & commercials. I waited for them to come to the right conclusion and when they were on the right track, I explained it more in depth to them. Example, comic #2 — Straw Man. I also admitted that I even struggle with finding this fallacy.	Instead of throwing up their hands and saying "Ms. Ross, I don't know," the students didn't give up on trying to figure out which fallacy was represented in the 2nd comic. They used the extra detail I gave them to lead them in the direction of the right answer.	When [Ada] still wasn't sure after the Kay Hagan commercial, she asked for clarification. She asked, "What's the difference between slippery slope and hasty generalization?"
Example two:	After we watched the first commercial, they gave me the right answer—Bandwagon. I asked them to give me more, tell me specific reasons why it was a bandwagon fallacy.	When I asked the class if they understood why comic #3 was a hasty generalization, Aaron spoke up and said he didn't get it.	The students wanted to branch off into a discussion about fallacies within the media (which we did, but it cut out of the video). They used my comments as a springboard for deeper discussion of their own.
Example three:	After we watched the Kay Hagan commercial, they weren't getting the answer that I wanted them to, but they were making great observations. Instead of just giving it to them and moving on, I gave them more details which helped them arrive at the right conclusion.	After the first commercial, the students offered specific reasons why the answer was slippery slope after I asked them.	After the Kay Hagan commercial, Jasmine asked, "So did they just choose Sheila Salter at random and tell her what to say or tell her story about Obama?" and craved more understanding about how fallacies are so prevalent in the media.

REFERENCES

Alsup, J. (2006). *Teacher identity discourses: Negotiating personal and professional spaces*. Mahwah, NJ: Lawrence Erlbaum.

Balfanz, R., & Byrnes, V. (2012). *The importance of being there: A report on absenteeism in the nation's public schools*. Baltimore, MD: Johns Hopkins University School of Education, Everyone Graduates Center, Get Schooled, 1–46.

Balfanz, R., & Legters, N. (2004). *Locating the dropout crisis: Which high schools produce the nation's Dropouts? Where are they located? Who attends them? Report 70*. Johns Hopkins: Center for Research on the Education of Students Placed at Risk (CRESPAR).

Cochran-Smith, M. (2004). *Walking the road: Race, diversity, and social justice in teacher education*. New York: Teachers College Press.

Darling-Hammond, L. (2010). Teacher education and the American future. *Journal of Teacher Education*, 61(1–2), 35–47.

Gay, G. (2010). *Culturally responsive teaching*. New York, NY: Teachers College Press.

González, N., Moll, L. C., & Amanti, C. (Eds.). (2013). *Funds of knowledge: Theorizing practices in households, communities, and classrooms*. New York, NY: Routledge.

Haniford, L. (2010). Tracing one teacher candidate's discursive identity work. *Teaching and Teacher Education*, 26, 987–996.

Juzwik, M. M. (2006). Performing curriculum: Building ethos through narrative in pedagogical discourse. *Teachers College Record*, 108(4), 489–528.

Kea, C. D., Trent, S. C., & Davis, C. P. (2002). African American student teachers' perceptions about preparedness to teach students from culturally and linguistically diverse backgrounds. *Multicultural Perspectives*, 4(1), 18–25.

Lazar, A. M., Edwards, P. A., & McMillon, G. T. (2012). *Bridging literacy and equity: The essential guide to social equity teaching*. New York, NY: Teachers College Press.

Levine-Rasky, C. (2000). Framing whiteness: Working through the tensions in introducing whiteness to educators. *Race, Ethnicity and Education*, 3(3), 271–292.

McIntyre, A. (1997). *Making meaning of Whiteness: Exploring racial identity with White teachers*. Albany, NY: State University of New York Press.

Sexton, D. M. (2008). Student teachers negotiating identity, role and agency. *Teacher Education Quarterly*, Summer, 73–88.

Sleeter, C. (2008). Critical family history, identity, and historical memory. *Educational Studies: Journal of the American Educational Studies Association*, 43(2), 114–124.

Smagorinsky, P., Cook, L. S., Moore, C., Jackson, A. Y., & Fry, P. G. (2004). Tensions in learning to teach: Accommodation and the development of a teaching identity. *Journal of Teacher Education*, 55(1), 8–24.

Vetter, A., Meacham, M., & Schieble, M. (2013). Leveling the field: Negotiating positions of power as a preservice teacher. *Action In Teacher Education*, 35(4), 230–251.

Villegas, A. M., & Irvine, J. J. (2010). Diversifying the teaching force: An examination of major arguments. *The Urban Review*, 42(3), 175–192.

5 Positions of Facilitative Teaching

In this chapter, we explore how one preservice teacher examined positions of facilitative teaching during her time as a student teacher. To begin, we provide a brief scenario. In a ninth-grade English classroom, Jaina's students read *The Scarlet Ibis* by James Hurst, a story about Brother, who recounts the life of his younger brother (Doodle) who was born sickly and not expected to live. Brother resented weak and fragile Doodle because he wanted someone to run and play with. With the goal of facilitating discussion about Doodle, Jaina asked an open-ended question: "If *The Scarlet Ibis* was told as if Doodle was the main narrator . . . would he be reliable?" From that question, students responded with various answers. Each time a student responded, Jaina evaluated the response and elicited more participation through other questions and connections, as illustrated in the following excerpt:

> **Demetra:** Because he is imaginative and it would not be straight up. He would be like, "Oh birds were flying in the sky," and he would make it imaginative.
> **Jaina:** Okay. It would be too imaginative. Okay. Good job. Terry?
> **Terry:** It would be confusing 'cause he's not really in his right mind, so he'd be going off topic.
> **Jaina:** Right.

From this short interaction, we noticed that Jaina's open-ended question elicited a thoughtful comment from Demetra because she elaborated with evidence from the text. In response, Jaina repeated her answer and evaluated with "Good job." She then invited Terry to participate, who added another perspective to the conversation. Jaina then responded with another evaluative comment ("Right"). Such Initiate-Respond-Evaluate (IRE) patterns continued throughout the rest of Jaina's transcribed video-recorded lesson focused on her teaching. Although it was her desire to take on a facilitator identity, we recognize that more could be done to invite student responses and foster thinking through talk.

This type of IRE pattern was typical in the video-recorded lessons of our preservice teachers. Despite the frequent use of that pattern, our teacher candidates often stated in their teaching philosophy that facilitating student learning through discussion was a desired position they hoped to enact in daily classroom interactions. As they attempted to facilitate student-centered, higher order classroom talk, they recognized that enacting a facilitative teacher identity was much more complex than they expected. From research, we know that novice teachers often employ IRE (Initiation-Response-Evaluation) patterns (Mehan, 1979) as a means of maintaining control and covering content, even though they desire not to do so. These behaviors are both a part of their own socialization histories with school-based language practices and are still highly visible in their intern opportunities in schools. Classroom dialogue, however, is important because it engages adolescents in higher order and critical thinking that is strongly linked to academic literacy development (Applebee, Langer, Nystrand, & Gamoran, 2003; Murphey et al., 2009). Being a successful facilitator of student talk requires teachers to be careful and purposeful navigators of classroom interactions that position students as capable literacy learners (Allwright, 1980; Cazden, 2001; Mercer, 2000; Rex & Schiller, 2009). Such navigations are linked to dialogic teaching, which refers to "instructional designs and practices that provide students with frequent and sustained opportunities to engage in learning talk" (Juzwik, Borsheim-Black, Caughlan, & Heintz, 2013).

Based on these dilemmas, it was clear to us that our students would benefit from exploring the complexities of a facilitator identity. Jaina's case study does just that.

In this chapter, we investigate the following questions:

- In what ways did Jaina construct and enact a facilitator identity?
- How did those constructions and enactments shape interactive and reflective positionings in one video-recorded lesson?
- In what ways did video analysis engage Jaina in reflection about her facilitator identity?

DIALOGIC INSTRUCTION

The centrality of classroom discourse to literacy development has much empirical and conceptual grounding in literacy research (Cazden, 2001). Teachers' questioning strategies that are open-ended and invite students to respond to one another have been linked to increased engagement and academic achievement (Applebee et al., 2003; Marshall, Smagorinsky, & Smith, 1995). Additionally, teachers' oral narratives have been shown to act as resources for inviting a multiplicity of student voices in response to literature (Juzwik, Nystrand, Kelly, & Sherry, 2008). Bakhtin and his colleagues (known as the Bakhtin Circle) developed a theory of language and meaning that conceptually informed this body of research. They theorized that any utterance (oral or written) simultaneously refracts a multitude of voices and anticipates a response from others—a process Bakhtin termed addressivity (ibid). Thus, language is understood as dialogic and mediated by purpose, relationships, and experience among interlocutors. The tension and interplay of these convergent meanings also allows for spontaneity and improvisation for new meanings to be made. Thus, a dialogic vision of classroom talk engages multiple students' voices and thrives on the conflict and tension of competing experience and interpretation.

However, researchers of classroom discourse have also found that much of school talk is authoritative or monologic—where one speaker's voice (the teacher's) is privileged (Nystrand, Gamoran, Kachur, & Prendergast, 1997). Classroom instruction characterized as monologic becomes a guessing game where the teacher determines the questions to be asked, students respond with the "right" answer that the teacher already possesses, and the teacher evaluates the response. This pattern is less cognitively demanding for students than dialogically organized instruction. Dialogic teaching is a teaching stance that aims to stimulate learning through talk rather than use talk as a way to display students' knowledge about a topic. In a dialogic classroom, teachers "optimize the dialogic potential of classroom discourse and discussion by opening the floor to student ideas and authorizing competing voices" (Juzwik et al., 2008, p. 1114). The process is facilitated by validating students' multiple contributions, practicing uptake—asking follow up questions to keep the discourse open for new perspectives—and asking authentic questions (Nystrand & Gamoran, 1991) that do not have a pre-specified response. Such dialogue is cognitively demanding for students because it invites their perspectives, connections, analyses, and questions. It is through this kind of dialogue that learning occurs (Barnes, Britton, & Torbe, 1986). Dialogic instruction also meets the needs of diverse populations because it inherently positions "individual students' cultures and backgrounds [as] essential ingredients in the construction of discourse-based knowledge" (Elizabeth, Anderson, Snow, & Selman, 2012, p. 1216). For preservice and novice teachers, it is important for them to learn how to take an authoritative stance while also fostering dialogue that allows students to contribute to the direction of classroom talk (Juzwik et al., 2013).

Research also illustrates that dialogic instruction improves literacy learning, especially as it relates to reading comprehension, engagement, and literary analysis (Applebee et al., 2003; Nystrand et al., 1991). Although the benefits to dialogic instruction are clear, we rarely see them in practice (Nystrand et al., 1997). This may be because teachers have yet to examine their facilitation skills and the ways in which those skills shape learning through talk in their classroom. For example, Elizabeth et al. (2012) conducted micro- and macro-analyses of classroom talk in response to read-alouds in the upper elementary grades. Their study aimed to characterize quality academic discussion, which a review of the literature supported as including "perspective taking, strong reasoning skills, an ability to connect factual knowledge to the topic, and an embracing attitude toward newly introduced ideas" (p. 1218). They found that whereas the teachers in the study characterized the classroom talk as improved in academic scope, their analyses of classroom transcripts showed otherwise.

To address those concerns, the Video-Based Response and Revision (VBRR), as mentioned in chapter two, uses video and web-based social networking resources to foster dialogic teaching. Specifically, this group uses collaborative video analysis to transform developing practices that push back against monologic interactions (i.e., teacher directed). By reviewing and responding to video-recorded interactions, Juzwik, Sherry, Caughlan, Heintz, and Borsheim-Black (2012) found that teacher candidates were more likely to recognize and transform monologic approaches to teaching. Overall, this approach has proven to be an effective strategy for disrupting counterproductive teaching practices that have the potential to become habitual.

Our concern as teacher educators reflects these findings—that our preservice English teachers desire to act as facilitators of dialogic discourse, yet they struggle to align this desired identity with classroom practice. We argue that more research needs to be done to find effective tools and strategies to help preservice teachers enact teacher identities that invite students' voices and develop their academic literacies. In particular, we believe that becoming interactionally aware of how one facilitates student-centered talk is a complex task that requires conceptual understanding, practice, patience, and tools for noticing, analyzing, and modifying language use in the classroom. Thus, we use the concept of dialogic teaching (Juzwik et al., 2013) as a framework for understanding the idea of facilitation that our teacher candidates discussed in our study. Because Jaina used the term facilitator throughout her teaching philosophy and video analysis, however, we use facilitator rather than dialogic instructor to describe a teacher who fosters opportunities for students to learn through open-ended discussion. Thus, we believe that a facilitator is recognized as one who promotes higher-level thinking by asking authentic questions that foster student participation, builds on student responses, and fosters dialogue that has continuity, coherence, and is "predominantly carried along by the students" (Elizabeth et al., 2012, p. 1220). In particular, we came to this study with an understanding of a facilitator as a guide who assists students through the process of co-constructing knowledge based on the multiplicities of students' experiences, cultural backgrounds, and reader transactions with a text. From this definition, we imagined a student-centered classroom in which students build knowledge through dialogue or problem-based learning in ways that reflected the critical pedagogy discussed in our courses. To explore how a preservice teacher attempts to take on a facilitator identity, we examine a transcript from one of Jaina's video-recorded lessons, along with her video analysis.

JAINA'S DESIRED TEACHING IDENTITIES: FACILITATIVE TEACHER

Jaina, an African American female in her early twenties, finalized her fieldwork at Lincoln High School (LHS), which was founded in 1929 as the first black high school in the county. During desegregation, the school population integrated and currently consists of a diverse student enrollment with a predominantly African American population of students. At the time of the study, a majority of African American students (95%), and Latino/as students (4%) attended LHS. Sixty-four percent of students were eligible for free or reduced lunch and 68% were proficient or above on the English state mandated exam (state average 81%).

We selected Jaina because she explicitly stated in her teaching philosophy and video analysis assignments that she wanted to be a facilitator in the classroom. Specifically, on her teacher blog, she stated that a teacher was one who "invites sharing of ideas, serves as guide, and creates spaces for students to grow intellectually, emotionally, and socially." She wanted to foster "a sense of community/togetherness in the classroom and serve as a guide to overcome roadblocks." All of this language situated Jaina as a facilitator who urged a student-centered classroom by inviting, sharing, and guiding students within a literacy community. Although Jaina does not use the term dialogic teaching, we believe that her verbs (*invite, share, create, facilitate*) connect with the concept of utilizing instructional moves to foster talk that supports learning in her classroom.

POSITIONS OF FACILITATIVE TEACHING

To illustrate Jaina's identity work as a facilitator, we organize our findings in two major sections. First, we analyze a transcribed classroom interaction from the video assignment to examine how she did or did not position herself as a facilitator. Second, we examine how she made sense of those positions in her written analysis about the transcription to illustrate how the assignment did or did not help her align her preferred teacher identities.

Posing Questions and Responding to Students

During an English I (ninth-grade) class period, Jaina recorded a lesson that focused on facilitating a discussion about the tone, mood, and other short story elements of *The Scarlet Ibis*. At the beginning of this transcript, Jaina picked up a quick-write assignment focused on point of view related to the questions she asked in this discussion. Throughout the following section, Jaina elicited conversation based on a central question about Doodle being a reliable narrator, some of which was in the opening scenario.

Jaina: . . . Okay. "The Scarlet Ibis" was about who?
Students: Doodle.
Jaina: Doodle. So, if *The Scarlet Ibis* was told as if Doodle was the main narrator, okay, would he be reliable?
Students: Nope. No.
Jaina: Or an unreliable narrator?
Students: Unreliable.
Jaina: Unreliable. Why? [Students begin shouting answers]. Okay, wait. Demetra?
Demetra: Because he is imaginative and it would not be straight up. He would be like, "Oh birds were flying in the sky," and he would make it imaginative.
Jaina: Okay. It would be too imaginative. Okay. Good job. Terry?
Terry: It would be confusing 'cause he's not really in his right mind, so he'd be going off topic.
Jaina: Right. Now in the story they said that Doodle was not what? All . . .
Students: There. Together.
Jaina: There. All there is an example of what? It starts with an "I." An . . . [Students begin shouting out incorrect answers].
Jaina: It starts with an "I." All there is an example of an id . . .
Sierra: Idiom.
Jaina: Idiom. Yes! Good job, Sierra. Yes. Another idiom would be, it's raining cats and dogs, or I heard it through the grapevine. Those are idioms. It really can't rain cats and dogs outside, but if you said it everybody knows exactly what you mean. But it is not to be taken literally. So, we have that Doodle might be an unreliable narrator because his imagination is too broad. Then Terry said that it would be too much confusion because he's not all there.

From this transcript, we take note of Jaina's questioning and response patterns in an effort to understand how she situated herself as a facilitator. Specifically, we examined if her questions were designed to provoke thoughtful response rather than recitation from students. At first, Jaina used known-answer/test questions to ensure that students understand that Doodle was the main character of the story. Although this is meant to facilitate interaction, the posed question expects a response from students and then elicits an evaluation from the teacher (i.e., confirmation through repetition of answer). This positioned Jaina as the knowledgeable figure in the interaction and students as passive receivers of that knowledge. Rather than facilitate dialogue, then, this approach fostered a more lecture-based learning space.

Next, Jaina asked two closed-ended questions (i.e., "Would Doodle be a reliable or unreliable character?") that led to an open-ended question by asking why students think Doodle is an unreliable character, as they indicated from earlier answers. Such an authentic question asked students to deliberate without there being one known answer. After Demetra answered with specific reasons related from the story, Jaina restated her comment and evaluated it (i.e., "Good job"). After Terry answered with another perspective, Jaina evaluated his answer (i.e., "Right") and asked a known-answer/test question about specific character traits of Doodle (i.e., "Not all there"). Although she used Terry's response as a building block to elaborate on his comment, she led into another known-answer question that asked students to guess what she was thinking (i.e., "It starts with an I"). After Sierra said the correct answer, she evaluated with a "Good job" moving back into teacher talk by elaborating on the importance of idioms in literature. Although it is not clear if this was Jaina's goal all along, it does appear that she attempted to take advantage of a teaching moment (in regards to figurative language) by building on Terry and students' comments about Doodle not being all there. At the same time, after two student responses, Jaina quickly redirected the conversation back to a more teacher-led discussion. Such a move could position students less as learning through talk and more as passive listeners of teacher talk, particularly if done consistently throughout the discussion. Overall, Jaina positioned herself as a facilitator by asking an open-ended, authentic question regarding students' thoughts. Through redirection, recitation, and teacher talk, however, she repositioned herself more as a director rather than a facilitator of student talk. By doing this, her students were situated as passive learners rather than active learners who learn from each other, a scenario that contradicts Jaina's goal of facilitating.

In the next excerpt, Jaina continues to ask students what they thought about Doodle being an unreliable narrator and responds in various ways to elicit more conversation.

> **Jaina:** And what else? What else? Who else said unreliable? Why else would Doodle be an unreliable narrator? He has too broad of an imagination. And . . .
> **Kia:** Could it be because he's too young?
> **Jaina:** He's not all there. Maybe because he's too young.
> **Angie:** He can't really talk right can he?
> **Jaina:** He can't talk that well. What else? What about Doodle? Go ahead Bryson.
> **Bryson:** He won't explain stuff very well as the narrator.
> **Jaina:** Right. He might not be able to explain things well as the narrator.
> **Kia:** And he dies.
> **Jaina:** And he dies, of course. But what might make him a reliable narrator?
> **Sierra:** Because it's being seen through his eyes. It's being told by him.
> **Jaina:** Right. He's the one telling the story if he is the narrator. What else? What is the story really about?

Students: Doodle.

Jaina: Doodle. The story is about him, so he might be reliable. How else could he possibly be reliable?

Bryson: You get better details and his point of view.

Jaina: Right. You might get better details from his point of view. So if we're pulling out things from the story . . . when Doodle got tipped over in the go-cart . . . maybe if Doodle was the narrator how might he explain that?

Demetra: He would say, "Oh my God I was in a spaceship on a rocket and fell."

Jaina: That's true. Demetra brought up a good point. Doodle did have what some people might consider a weird imagination, so he might have thought of the go-cart as a rocket or a spaceship or something. And maybe he might like getting tipped over.

In this section, Jaina asked students to continue the dialogue by asking several versions of the same authentic question ("What else?" or "Why else?"). She even restated Terry's answer to remind students of what had already been said. Next, Kia asked a question about the possibility of Doodle's age shaping his experience. Jaina then related that question to what was said earlier about Doodle not being all there. Although Jaina's intention was to keep the conversation going, by answering Kia's question, she shut down a possibility for others to build on Kia's comment. What might have happened if Jaina asked others how they could answer Kia's question? A similar pattern occurred when Angie posed a question about Doodle's ability to talk. Jaina repeated Angie's question and asked for more suggestions. Although she attempted to gain wide participation by asking for more suggestions, she missed an opportunity to extend on and facilitate in-depth responses in connection to the responses students were giving. Again, what might happen if Jaina asked others what they thought of Angie's question?

Jaina continued the pattern of recitation with Bryson and Kia in the next few lines. Although teachers often use recitation and evaluation as ways to sustain the conversation, such responses can shut down multiple perspectives and personal connections because they appear to be irrelevant. Thus, by evaluating, Jaina positioned students as right and wrong rather than fostering student talk that builds on each other's comments. A similar IRE pattern continued throughout the rest of the transcript. Overall, Jaina positioned herself as a facilitator by asking an authentic question and eliciting several responses from students. She risked, however, positioning students as being right or wrong by evaluating their comments. In addition, by reciting each person's response, she positioned herself as in control of the discussion rather than allowing students to pull the reigns every now and then. This contradicts notions of dialogic teaching that fosters student talk to inspire and expand students' thinking.

82   *Positions of Facilitative Teaching*

In the next excerpt, Jaina makes a connection between their conversation and a past lesson on characterization.

> **Jaina:** So, before when we started reading the story we did some characterization. We said that the narrator, we characterized him as what?
> **Damien:** Doodle's brother.
> **Jaina:** Well we know he's Doodle's brother, but was he nice, was he mean?
> **Damien:** Oh, mean. Mean.
> **Jaina:** He was mean. But then at the same time he had a what?
> **Damien:** Heart.
> **Jaina:** He had a heart. He cared a little bit. I mean, he did mean stuff to Doodle, but then he was like, "Dang, that was mean. I shouldn't have done that. That was mean." If Doodle was the narrator, how could we possibly characterize him? What do you think?
> **Sierra:** Nice, cool.
> **Alana:** Maybe nonchalant.
> **Jaina:** Yes, I almost passed out! She used a tone and mood word. Good job. Nonchalant! Good job, [Alana]. Okay, [Bryson]. Sorry. I had to give her a spotlight for a minute. Okay, go ahead. [Student and teacher laugh together for a second].
> **Bryson:** I was just going to say that he would probably be a nice person.
> **Jaina:** Right. Do you think that we would have ever seen an angry side of Doodle? I mean seriously?
> **Students:** No.
> **Jaina:** No. Why not?
> **Damien:** He's special.
> **Kia:** He wasn't all there.
> **Jaina:** Right. He wasn't all there. He thought that everything that his brother did was what?
> **Terry:** Good.
> **Jaina:** Normal. Out of love. Right. Okay, so we're going to go into point of view a little bit more in detail on Monday with some different stories I think you guys would like. So we'll talk about it more then.

In this excerpt, Jaina continued to use an IRE pattern while also attempting to build on past classroom conversations. For instance, when Damien answered one question, Jaina asked other known-answer questions to build up to an authentic question asking students what they think about characterizing Doodle as the narrator of the study. Here, her known-answer questions built on past conversations to construct learning about a new idea. Thus, Jaina situated herself as a facilitator by asking an authentic question and attempting to build on students' responses (e.g., Bryson's response). The transcript, however, continues to follow an IRE pattern. Thus, by reciting and eliciting she risked situating students as passive listeners giving "correct" answers rather than engaging in dialogue to learn from each other.

Participation Patterns

To further examine how Jaina took on a facilitator identity, we examined the transcript as a whole. Specifically, we examined specific dialogic markers that are often used to help evaluate if a discussion is actually dialogic. Thus, we provide an overview of student and teacher participation patterns (Table 5.1) to illustrate how Jaina situated herself as a facilitator. In particular, we used Juzwik et al.'s (2013) suggestions for possible ways into dialogic classroom discourse analysis. From this analysis, we learned four points about the participation patterns of both Jaina and her students in this transcript. First, it is evident that both Jaina and her students engaged in the conversation (27 teacher moves and 24 student moves). Second, although some of Jaina's responses tended to be longer than student responses, overall responses were fairly even, another indication that Jaina situated herself as a facilitator and her students as participants in a dialogic classroom. Third, seven out of 29 students spoke in the transcript. This finding indicates that in order for Jaina to position all of her students as participants in the

Table 5.1 Participation Patterns

Teacher Moves	27
Student Moves	24
Length of teacher turns	Overall, the length of student and teacher talk is similar. There are three instances in which Jaina takes an extended time to talk.
How many students participated?	7/29 students spoke in this transcript
Which students participated?	No one student dominated the conversation. An even amount of boys and girls spoke (4 girls/3 boys).
What were the participation patterns?	Teacher—Student—Teacher—Student This was the common pattern throughout the transcript.
How did the teacher participate?	3 Teacher Authentic Questions (TAQ); 6 Teacher Nonauthentic Questions (TNQ); 0 Teacher Uptake (TU); 13 Responses (R); 0 Classroom Management (CM).
How did students participate?	Students spoke in phrases and short sentences. 2 questions; 1 response

Juzwik et al. (2013)

classroom discussion, she might need to find more ways to foster talk from her quieter students. Fourth, Jaina had two central questions in mind that elicited students' opinions about the story. One was in regards to Doodle being a reliable character and the other was in regards to Doodle being an unreliable character. Those two central questions tended to elicit the most student responses. Other questions that she posed were known-answer questions. This finding raised inquiries about how her question and response patterns shaped how she situated herself as a facilitator and her students as participants.

Jaina's Reflection: Posing Questions and Responding to Students

To explore how Jaina reflected about her facilitator identity, we examined her response to the above interactions from the first video analysis assignment. Throughout her video analysis, she discussed specific discourse patterns that related to how she took on a facilitator position and how those positionings situated students. To begin, we include an excerpt from her analysis that examines the kinds of questions she posed throughout the interaction:

> I noticed that I tend to form open-ended questions, and give them clues as to when and how I want them to answer the questions by having the word 'what' at the end of the question. I tend to revert to asking students questions that assess their knowledge of the material. The questions that I pose to the students usually begin or end with 'what,' how do you know, and 'what if.' . . . When I posed those types of questions, I facilitated one-word answers. Other times I would facilitate opinionated answers that displayed the students' basic knowledge of the material.

In the same sentence, Jaina used the phrase "open-ended questions" with "give them clues as to when and how I want them to answer." These contradictory phrases illustrate tension about what it means to enact a facilitator identity. At this point, Jaina described a facilitator as someone who guides students toward telling her the "correct" answer. This philosophy contradicts ideas of dialogic teaching that utilize authentic questions to foster student opinions in whatever form they choose (i.e., story, another question, connection). This is a common dilemma for teachers who want to practice dialogic teaching (Juzwik et al., 2013) while also preparing students for specific assessments (i.e., test). This challenge could also be related to Jaina's status as a novice teacher who also desired to, as explained in a blog entry after her first co-taught lesson, assert her authority. One way to do that is by illustrating knowledge about her content area. In fact, she stated, "I noticed that the students tend to position me as a scholarly teacher as well. The students rely on me to teach them ways to question and analyze literature."

Thus, having control over the direction of a conversation ensures that she will be positioned as the expert.

In the next paragraph, Jaina commented on a few positive aspects of her questioning techniques and then described specific ways she could make pedagogical changes.

> When I asked open-ended questions to the students I noticed that the students began to facilitate more discussion. One strength that I noticed during the video was my ability to assess the students' comprehension of the text via oral questioning. To focus on students as learners, I could have had all of the students share one main point from the text to assess students' comprehension of the text. Another strength that I noticed during the video was my ability to incorporate guided questions throughout the lesson. One way that I could improve that technique would be to incorporate words such as, "Explain," "Analyze," or "Interpret." Overall, I think that incorporating higher-level questioning words or phrases would help me understand my students as learners a little better. If I asked questions about analyzing and my students struggle to answer the questions, then I can make the assumption that they do not completely understand how to analyze.

Jaina's initial sentence stated that open-ended questions engaged students more in the discussion. Later in the reflection, she also noted that she could use words, such as "Analyze," to foster higher-level discussions. For Jaina, these are concrete ways for her to position students as learners through discussion. At this point, she recognized that open-ended questions needed to elicit student thought about a topic rather than search for a specific answer. Jaina also stated that one of her strengths is asking questions to assess learning, specifically comprehension. Again, to situate students as learners, she described the possibility of asking students to share a main idea from the text. This strategy could be more dialogic because it focuses on student answers, rather than asking pointed questions to elicit the "right" answer. Thus, Jaina noted specific strategies to foster learning through talk. At the same time, Jaina might miss some opportunities to foster such learning if her purpose of discussions is only assessment. When teachers assess through talk, they often engage in an IRE pattern of talk that stifles the learning that could occur from more student-rich talk. Her suggestion to ask students to share a main point from the text fosters student-centered participation, but could become a guessing game for the right answer if the end goal is assessment. Although assessment is an important aspect of teaching, it does not always need to be the sole purpose of discussion. In fact, dialogic teaching argues that teachers can understand what students know by fostering student-led conversation. However, that assessment might require a more experienced teacher who is able to assess knowledge in a less structured format.

Although pleased with some of her questioning techniques, she also noted, "Students seemed to have expected me to facilitate the discussions and sometimes it seemed as if they expected me to facilitate the answers to questions." From the phrase "facilitate the answers to questions," we understand that Jaina recognized that students were relying on her for the answers rather than developing their own. Her choice of the word "facilitate" rather than "tell" illustrated her shifting perception about what it meant to facilitate a discussion or learning. In other words, Jaina had difficulty enacting a facilitator identity that assisted students through the learning process by "sharing and inviting" perspectives. Instead, Jaina seemed most comfortable with a teacher identity that led students to pre-determined answers. The use of "questions" and "answers" portrayed her belief that a facilitator was one who asked questions and evaluated answers. At the same time, Jaina might have been attempting to portray an identity that she believed was most acceptable to her instructor or cooperating teacher (i.e., knowledge of content and control of the classroom). Jaina did, however, examine this issue when she used the term "rely" to convey her concern that students depended on her for the answers. She stated that she was not comfortable taking on that position, which, at this moment, challenged her to explore what it meant to facilitate learning.

She continued to examine that notion at the end of her reflection. Jaina stated:

> It is important for me to guide discussions so the students have a model of an effective academic discussion. I learned that in order to facilitate learning I have to ensure that I have a goal for the students to achieve. I have to know where my students are academically, where I want them to be over a certain period of time, and where I wanted to see myself as a teacher. . . . In order to facilitate learning I have to understand what I want my students to learn from me, but also what I want to learn from my students. I've learned to ask: "How did you come up with that answer," and "Why do you think that is correct?" Also, in order to keep the learning process interesting I incorporated various things into the lesson that would keep them interested such as music lyrics, television shows, art, etc.

In this example, Jaina described a facilitator identity as a teacher who has clear direction and teaches students particular concepts (i.e., a teacher-centered approach). She also said that a facilitator identity is a teacher who learns from students and incorporates music lyrics or television shows into her lessons to interest students. Thus, her description vacillated between teacher-centered actions ("understand what I want students to know from me") to student-centered actions ("keep the learning process interesting, know where my students are academically"). This vacillation illustrated her belief that a facilitator has specific goals for students to reach and her job is to guide them toward those goals by understanding their academic backgrounds and making it interesting for students.

To end, we share Jaina's final sentences from her reflection. These reflective statements continue to illustrate her developing understanding of what it means to enact a facilitator identity.

> I believe that students positioned me as the facilitator during this lesson. . . . Students knew that there was a certain concept that I wanted them to learn during the lesson and they trusted me enough to believe that I was going to thoroughly teach them what I wanted them to learn.

Similar to her own positionings, Jaina illustrated that students situated her as a facilitator who directed them toward a "certain concept" and taught them what she wanted them to learn. This can be empowering for novice teachers who are striving to gain authority in the classroom and be respected teachers by colleagues. A dialogic teacher is someone who is purposeful and designs with specific goals in mind. Jaina desired to promote whole-group collaboration and facilitate a space in which students shared without fear of getting the answer wrong (Alexander, 2008). However, Jaina also missed opportunities to help students build on ideas and connect individual contributions into sustained and coherent talk about curriculum. To entertain more robust understandings of what it means to be a facilitator, Jaina would have benefitted from examining how dialogue is reciprocal, in that teachers and students share ideas in response to and in anticipation of the ideas of others.

FINAL THOUGHTS

As mentioned, Jaina wanted to situate herself as a "guide" who fostered the "sharing of ideas" in a community that supported students' growth "intellectually, emotionally, and socially." In her video analysis, Jaina engaged in reflection about how she enacted a facilitator identity and she noted specific ways that she could improve that enactment (i.e., more participation). Thus, Jaina developed new ways of noticing aspects of classroom interactions through video analysis and how those interactions relate to her identity work as a teacher (i.e., that students recognize her as the keeper of knowledge). Teacher candidates oftentimes have difficulty situating themselves as the kind of teachers they hope to become during internships and student teaching. This is understandable given their novice status and the pressures they have to enact teacher identities that will ensure success within the university and the public school institution.

Specifically, this analysis challenged Jaina to define what she meant by a facilitator identity. In her philosophy, she begins with a broad statement about students sharing ideas and building a community of growth. Through close analysis of her transcript, she developed a more concrete understanding of a facilitator as someone who guides students in a purposeful direction related to literacy learning. For her, facilitation also included the evaluation and assessment of student ideas to ensure that they were learning. In addition, Jaina examined what it meant to enact a facilitator identity. Through this exploration, she discovered a few dilemmas. First, she noticed that the kinds of questions posed (open-ended versus closed-ended) matter. Second, she realized that making connections to the lives of students likely engaged them more in discussion. Third, she became aware of how students recognized her; she held the knowledge and students expected her to guide them in the "right" direction.

We recognize, however, that Jaina needed more guidance in examining how her teacher philosophy conflicted with or contributed to their enactments, especially as it related to enacting her desired pedagogy. For example, she stated that she wanted to foster student-centered dialogue in her class, but when she attempted to enact that identity, discussions resulted in continuous IRE patterns (Nystrand & Gamoran, 1991) that were not noted or disrupted by Jaina's analysis. She did, however notice that she could have asked more higher level questions and that open-ended questions tended to elicit more student participation and engagement. To foster Jaina's identity work in this area, we understand that our students needed more opportunities to deconstruct what it means to take on a facilitator identity. Thus, when students write about the kind of teacher identities they hope to take up, teacher education courses could first ask students to read and learn about what those identities might entail. Perhaps teacher candidates might be more prepared to position themselves in ways that align with those identities and recognize moments when misalignments occur.

IT'S YOUR TURN: EXPLORING POSITIONS OF DIALOGIC TEACHING

To further illustrate how teachers can use discourse analysis to examine the enactment of a facilitator identity, let's look at a transcript from Tim's high school creative writing classroom.

Tim, a student teacher who desired to take on facilitator identities, student taught at a public school with an academy for the arts. To teach creative writing, he used a writing workshop format that focused on writing as a process. On this day, students were asked to read aloud a story they made on Storybird (a visual storytelling website). The class was asked to listen and provide feedback focused on successes and areas of improvement. As you read, think about the following questions: In what ways did Tim use talk to situate himself as a facilitator? How did he position his students? How did they position him? Use Tables 5.2 and 5.3 for support in examining language.

Table 5.2 Analysis Chart for Positions of Facilitative Teaching

Evidence from transcript (list transcript lines or describe interaction).	Reflexive Positioning: In what ways did Tim position himself as a facilitator for students?	Interactive Positioning: In what ways did Tim position his students as participants?	Interactive Positioning: In what ways did students position Tim as a facilitator?

Table 5.3 Analysis Guide for Dialogic Teaching

Teacher Moves
Student Moves
Length of teacher turns
How many students participated?
Which students participated?
What were the participation patterns?
How did the teacher participate?
How did students participate?

Juzwik et al. (2013)

> **Tim (teacher):** Okay so now we're going to share our Storybirds we've been working on. At the end of everyone's Storybird, we're going to do a little bit of feedback: something we saw we liked, something that is an area for improvement, and then hopefully we'll be able to go back and work on some more Storybirds this week and the beginning of next week and bring in stuff we talked about. Okay? I think Lane is going to go first since he had two Storybirds to share.
>
> **Lane:** [Reads *The Scary Mansion's Stories*. His story is about a werewolf, mummy, witch, and ghost who are being chased by a mean dog named Marvin. They humorously try to scare him away with their magical powers.]
>
> **Tim:** Okay, so now we're going to start sharing some stuff we liked about it. What did you guys like?

Berry: Um, I thought the story was kind of cute. It was interesting how you took the haunted house characters and made them kind of dorky.

Samantha: I like the characterization of each character. Each had their own personality that you got across in the short time.

Tim: I also liked the kind of personalities, like Samantha said, the kind of personalities you put into them are all unique. I can hear the personalities that you put into them; I can hear your voice, but they have their own voice as well. Not only did you see individual personalities, but you saw her personality as well. What kind of stuff did you see she could improve on for the next Storybird?

Berry: The actual way you wrote it, I don't think it worked—it would have worked better for a short animation. For the book format, there was a lot of back and forth dialogue and pictures being repeated and that kind of thing.

Samantha: I feel like there were sound effects that you put in that weren't really necessary . . . because when people read, you would pick up on that. And I feel like we realize he was tired—you could say he was trying to catch his breath, like "Fred was trying to catch his breath . . ."

Berry: Yeah, instead of puff in parenthesis over and over again, you could have just put dot dot dot.

Tim: I think—I feel that this Storybird was more of a children's novel, so I think some more direct characterization—so telling the kids what the personality is going to be instead of letting them infer from the indirect characterization—would be a way to make it more accessible to the children who read it—but it was really good. I really enjoyed it.

In response to this transcript, we discuss our thoughts on how Tim used language to position himself and his students in relation to dialogic teaching. For the following discussion, we take note of how students either take up or resist those positionings and what those positionings did for Tim's goals as a teacher.

We recognize that Tim situated himself as a dialogic teacher by creating a specific focus and structure for the discussion related to writing (e.g., strengths and areas of improvement). This provides an explicit format in which students can speak for this activity. Although structure can sometimes be stifling, when it comes to providing feedback for writing, specific guidelines typically produce more constructive suggestions. Tim also positioned himself as facilitator by fostering opportunities for students to share their writing and provide feedback to each other. By doing this, Tim situated students as writers and the entire class as a writing community dedicated to improving each other's work. Finally, Tim positioned himself as a facilitator by engaging in feedback that follows the guidelines he set. By waiting for others to start, he situated himself as a participant rather than an evaluator. With that said, we notice that only three students contributed to the conversation. Without knowing more about the students in the classroom, it is difficult to explain the lack of participation. It is clear, however, that more students need to be involved in order for a classroom community to be built.

How does Tim leverage these concepts to make sense of his classroom interactions? Although the transcript provides some insight into dialogic teaching in this classroom, Tim's reflection provides important context for a more constructive interpretation. Thus, we begin with Tim's response about participation patterns in his transcript:

> The students do most of the talking throughout this lesson. I think that I speak to the students in an adult way; I spoke as if we were peers in the process, but I also made sure to use language that was important to have in mind as they were growing in their awareness of the writing process. As for directives, I tended to use "we" language but that also made the most sense because I was participating in the process as well. As stated, I structured it so that praises and criticisms were lumped so that it was easier to process for the person who was receiving the feedback. I make it a point to treat all my students as writers. I think the language that I chose reflected this, as I had it as a class-wide writing workshop, which is a huge part of being a community of learners. The students and I were positioned as equal, except when I introduced what we were doing. I attempted to set the groundwork from the very beginning for what was to be expected so that it would flow most smoothly and allowed the students to follow the process that I explained in the beginning.

From Tim's analysis, we understand that he intentionally situated himself as a participant in the feedback process by talking less than his students, speaking as a peer when giving feedback, and using the pronoun *we*. At the same time, he noted that his facilitator position included language that guided students' awareness of the writing process. He also noted that he provided a set structure for the students so that the student writers could easily process the feedback discussion. Thus, for Tim, he took on a facilitator identity by positioning himself as a peer and a guide.

Tim also observed that only a small number of students participated, which he examines in his reflection.

> As for improvement, not all of my students participated. The class we're looking at is actually a very small creative writing class. I had one student manning the camera, so I think he felt like he shouldn't speak so

> as not to overpower the camera. He's normally very opinionated. I have another student, but she tends to err on the silent side, so next time I might require all students to provide feedback, instead of just opening the floor for feedback. I question this, though, as forced feedback might take away from the legitimacy of what is shared and becomes finding something to say because it is required, not because it's truly noteworthy.

Here, Tim discussed the need for more students to become involved in the discussion. He attempted to gain an understanding of why students did not participate by listing reasons, such as a small class, one vocal student focusing on the camera, and one typically quiet student. For future plans to situate students as participants, he suggested that he could require everyone to provide verbal feedback. Tim is not convinced, however, that is the best solution because he fears that students could give feedback just for the sake of giving feedback. This is an interesting dilemma to bring up because it illustrates how positionings are complicated when teachers are not confident about their instructional decisions. For some reason, students resisted the position of members of a writing community by not giving feedback. This raises questions about how teachers can situate students as participative members who learn about writing through collaborative talk.

Tim also recognized that past experiences shaped his identity work as a facilitator. In particular, he discussed that his school background played a part in this teaching style and he confirms that his enactments aligned with his philosophy as a teacher.

> I feel very comfortable leading group discussions because I often did that while learning myself. This is actually pretty accurately aligned with what I want to be as a teacher. I love discussion. I love group work and I love students getting to show off the work they accomplish. Communal learning is a huge part of my philosophy.

Here, Tim noted that he was comfortable with classroom discussions because that is how he learned in high school as well. He is aware that his positionings during this lesson align with his goal of being a facilitator focused on communal learning. Specifically, he highlights enjoying discussion, group work, and fostering opportunities for students to show off the work they accomplish. After reading Tim's transcript and analysis, do you agree with his final thoughts? Why or why not? What are your ideas about how Tim might foster participation, utilize authentic questions, and build on student ideas during dialogue focused on improving writing? What might hinder these discourse patterns from situating students as members of a writing community?

REFERENCES

Alexander, R. (2008). *Essays on pedagogy*. London, UK: Routledge.
Allwright, R. L. (1980). Turns, topics, and tasks: Patterns of participation in language learning and teaching. In D. Larsen-Freeman (Ed.), *Discourse analysis in second language research* (pp. 165–187). Rowley, MA: Newbury House.
Applebee, A., Langer, J., Nystrand, M., & Gamoran, A. (2003). Discussion based approaches to developing understanding: Classroom instruction and student performance in middle and high school English. *American Educational Research Journal, 40*(3), 685–730.
Barnes, D. R., Britton, J. N., & Torbe, M. (1986). *Language, the learner and the school*. New York: Penguin.
Cazden, C. (2001). *Classroom discourse: The language of teaching and learning*. Portsmouth, NH: Heinemann.
Elizabeth, T., Anderson, T., Snow, E., & Selman, R. (2012). Academic discussions: An analysis of instructional discourse and an argument for an integrative assessment framework. *American Educational Research Journal, 49*(6), 1214–1250.
Juzwik, M. M., Borsheim-Black, C., Caughlan, S., & Heintz, S. (2013). *Inspiring dialogue: Talking to learn in the English classroom*. New York, NY: Teachers College Press.
Juzwik, M. M., Nystrand, M., Kelly, S., & Sherry, M. (2008). Oral narrative genres as dialogic resources for classroom literature study: A contextualized case study. *American Educational Research Journal, 45*, 1111–1154.
Juzwik, M. M., Sherry, M. B., Caughlan, S., Heintz, A., & Borsheim-Black, C. (2012). Supporting dialogically organized instruction in an English teacher preparation program: A video-based, Web 2.0-mediated response and revision pedagogy. *Teachers College Record, 114*(3), 1–42.
Marshall, J. D., Smagorinsky, P., & Smith, M. W. (1995). *The language of interpretation: Patterns of discourse in discussions of literature*. NCTE Research Report No. 27. Urbana, IL: National Council of Teachers of English.
Mehan, H. (1979). *Learning lessons: Social organization in the classroom*. Cambridge, MA: Harvard University Press.
Mercer, N. (2000). *Words and minds: How we use language together*. London: Routledge.
Murphy, P. K., Wilkinson, I. A. G., Soter, A. O., Hennessey, M. N., & Alexander, J. F. (2009). Examining the effects of classroom discussion on students' high-level comprehension of text: A meta-analysis. *Journal of Educational Psychology, 101*(3), 740–764.
Nystrand, M., & Gamoran, A. (1991). Instructional discourse, student engagement, and literature achievement. *Research in the Teaching of English, 25*(3), 261–290.
Nystrand, M., Gamoran, N., Kachur, R., & Prendergast, C. (1997). *Opening dialogue: Understanding the dynamics of language and learning in the English classroom*. New York, NY: Teachers College Press.
Rex, L., & Schiller, L. (2009). *Using discourse analysis to improve classroom interaction*. New York, NY: Routledge.

6 Positions of Critical and Racial Literacy

Contributing Author: Mark Meacham

Chapters Three through Five focus on case studies that examine how one preservice teacher used the video analysis assignment to investigate his or her desired teaching identities. We take this chapter in a slightly different direction based on findings from across our case studies. Overall, our research uncovered that participants would have benefitted from more self-reflection and critical insight about how identity markers (e.g., race, class, gender, sexual orientation, ability, etc.) shaped teacher positionings. Rather than focus solely on the videos of classroom teaching as in previous chapters, this chapter examines the conversations that occurred among participants about the video analysis assignment in Amy and Mark's student teaching seminar to investigate these very issues that occurred two years after Amy and Melissa's study described in other chapters. Mark was a doctoral student in English Education. At the time he was co-teaching English Methods and the student teaching seminar with Amy.

To open, we present a short excerpt from Tammy, who described her difficulty discussing how identity markers shaped her teacher identities. This comment occurred during the seminar when teacher candidates met to discuss their video projects. Before Tammy's comment, Amy and Mark modeled a conversation for the group based on a video-recorded transcript they analyzed from the semester before in their English Methods course. To begin, they viewed the video-recorded section. Next, Amy and Mark reviewed a series of questions on the board that they expected students to discuss in small groups. One of those questions asked them to specifically address the following: In what ways does your race, class, gender, and sexual orientation shape your teacher positionings? This question was included in the original video assignment, but Mark and Amy felt that students needed more scaffolding to address the complexities of this question than was initially provided. Amy and Mark modeled what that conversation could look like by discussing the questions in regards to their transcript while students watched. Students then gathered in pairs to discuss their own video-recorded lessons. After their small group discussion, we debriefed about their conversations as a whole group. Toward the end of that discussion, Tammy (African American, middle-class, female) said the following:

> Um, in the written part, I had a really hard time answering the question about race, class, gender. I told Emma in the beginning that I don't even

pay attention to all of that when I'm teaching. I thought it was about respect and about love and teaching and all that, but listening to her response made me think more about it and I'm like hmmm, how does it really affect me in the classroom and my kids and their interactions. And I said that maybe the reason some of them treat me the way they do is because I'm like that missing thing that they don't have. A lot of my kids come from that "other" background. A lot of them are in foster care or something like that and they are being raised by an aunt or an older sister. So maybe I'm like that African American strong Black lady that's missing.

For us, this comment was significant because Tammy, who student taught in a predominately African American school, explicitly stated how the assignment and small group conversation helped her to understand how her race, class, and gender shaped how students positioned her as a teacher. Although Tammy's comment would benefit from multiple perspectives and critical questions that disrupt assumptions about students, openly discussing how markers of difference shape classroom interactions was not always easy for our students. In both courses, we noticed that students tended to ignore this question or deny that these identities impacted their pedagogy. As illustrated from the above excerpt, we were curious about the kind of supports (i.e., modeling dialogue, small group conversations) that might help to foster this kind of dialogue. To explore that dilemma, we asked the following question:

- In what ways did candidates examine how identity markers shaped teacher positionings through critical conversations about video-recorded lessons?

CRITICAL CONVERSATIONS IN TEACHER EDUCATION

Scholars that focus on meeting the needs of diverse student populations have argued that a homogeneous teacher workforce contributes to cultural misunderstandings between teachers and students (Ladson-Billings, 1991; McIntyre, 1997; Zeichner, 1993). For instance, Frederick, Cave, and Perencevich (2010) conducted a study of mostly White middle class teacher candidates enrolled in a Foundations of Education course. The study, which focused on shifts in teacher candidates' perspectives toward social inequity, found that many of the participants had little experience exploring issues associated with diversity or social justice prior to enrolling in the course. In order to address this need, teacher educators committed to this issue have explored the benefits of instructor-led discussions about race, class, gender, and sexual orientation (Chavez-Reyes, 2012; Cruz-Janzen, 2000; MacPherson, 2010; Mosley, 2010; Sleeter, Torres, & Laughlin, 2004). Findings in this area of research suggest that encouraging preservice teachers to draw on personal experience fosters their understandings about social difference (Depalma, 2010; Milner, 2006; Sleeter, 2011). In a study featuring a culturally diverse group of teacher candidates, Daniel (2009) noted that participants' sharing of prior experiences with racism and sexual discrimination fostered understandings of forms of oppression present in schools. According to the author, because participants drew on prior knowledge, classroom conversations became "a site of shared experience as a nexus of engagement with difference" (p. 184). Likewise, Depalma (2010) found that drawing on personal experience fostered participants' dialogic discussion about herteronormativity in both the classroom and in online discussion threads. Findings indicated that study participants used their personal experiences to extend and, in some cases, challenge ideas their fellow students shared about race and gender. In calling for classroom conversations about culture and race, Milner (2006) also argued that preservice teachers must be given opportunities to draw on "their own experiences, life worlds, privileges, struggles, and positions in relation to others" (p. 371).

Whereas previous studies suggest that examining personal experiences fosters meaningful dialogue, other studies indicate that modeling how one might engage in such interactions may further enrich understandings about social difference (Adler, 2011; Chavez-Reyes, 2012; Parker & Howard, 2009). For example, Chavez-Reyes (2012) described how she modeled Critical Social Dialogue (CSD) with a culturally diverse group of undergraduate students. According to the author, CSD involves active engagement in dialogue centered on social difference as well as ethical reasoning. In her courses, the author notes that modeling how one might share personal narratives and participate in active dialogue within a group setting helps move certain students from silence to engagement. Subsequently, as the semester progressed, more students engaged in discussions that resulted "in new considerations, insights or differences on social differences" (p. 49). Similarly, studies that draw on specific dimensions of critical literacy (e.g., disrupting the commonplace; interrogating multiple perspectives) to foster critical conversations between teachers and students suggest that such conversations provide a space for the critical analysis of race, class, gender, and sexual orientation, among other identity markers (Leland, Harste, Ociepka, Lewison, & Vasquez, 1999; Schieble, 2012b).

When considering how race, class, gender, and sexual orientation shape classroom interactions, research suggests that exploring identity markers may also foster preservice teachers' understandings of social difference (Mosley, 2010; Pewewardy, 2005; Sleeter, 2008). For instance, in a case study (2010) that featured a White female preservice teacher, Mosley found that the participant's involvement in book club discussions fostered racial literacy—or making sense of discursive and performative systems of race (Guinier, 2004). In her study, racial literacy focused on the critical examination of how White privilege functions within literacy practices. In particular, the participant used fictional texts to explore the role identity markers (e.g., White ally) play in taking an anti-racist stance. Mosley notes that such discussions may aid teachers in "design[ing] more just pedagogical spaces for students" (p. 469). However, Schieble (2012a) cautions that discussions exploring how identity markers shape interactions may not always result in greater understanding of social difference. Using critical discourse analysis to examine online discussion threads in a children's literature course, Schieble found that a pedagogical emphasis on politeness might, in fact, undermine preservice teachers' critical analyses of the role identity markers play in discussions of sexual orientation. Such a finding emphasizes the need for studies that further explore how teacher educators might foster classroom discussions that disrupt normative constructions of social difference.

Research indicates that small and whole group interactions may aid in teacher candidates' understandings of social difference, but should be carefully supported and examined for substantive critical analysis. When instructors model dialogic interactions and provide opportunities to draw on personal experience and explore positional identities, preservice teachers gain new insights. Despite evidence that supports such interactions, most studies exploring the use of video analysis with preservice teachers do so in regards to fostering awareness of teaching in general (Baecher & Kung, 2011; Sherin & van Es, 2009; Vetter, Meacham, & Schieble, 2013). To extend this research, we explore how teacher candidates examined the ways in which identity markers shaped teacher positionings through critical conversations (defined below) about video-recorded lessons.

PERSPECTIVES OF CRITICAL LITERACY AND RACIAL LITERACY

To examine how teachers engaged in such identity work through video analysis, we draw from the following interrelated theoretical perspectives: critical literacy (Janks, 2010) and racial literacy (Guinier, 2004). These theories offered specific ways in which to identify how preservice teachers engaged in dialogue about how identity markers shape teacher positions, which we call critical conversations (Fecho, Collier, Friese, & Wilson, 2010; Rogers & Christian, 2007; Smith, 2001). Stemming from critical pedagogy (McLaren, 1998), critical literacy takes an instructional approach that encourages and supports students as they read, analyze, critique, and question the messages inherently present within any form of text (Christensen, 2000). Practicing critical literacy means challenging themes of power and oppression in an attempt to expose how social and material ways of knowing privilege some perspectives and groups over others, often in ways that remain hidden and unseen (Janks, 2010). Such work potentially helps students develop a broader perspective of their social and cultural world and reflect on what it means to be an agent of change. For this study, we draw from Lewison, Flint, and Van Sluys (2002), who define critical literacy as having the following four dimensions: (a) disrupting the commonplace, (b) interrogating multiple viewpoints, (c) focusing on sociopolitical issues, and (d) taking action and promoting social justice. We use these four dimensions to better understand how preservice teachers engaged in dialogue about how markers of difference shaped their teacher identities.

Related to critical literacy, racial literacy sets out to develop an understanding of how race shapes the sociocultural experiences of individuals and groups (Skerrett, 2011, p. 314). In particular, the aim is to open opportunities for individuals to become more literate about how racism pervades our social, cultural, material, and political worlds (Guinier, 2004). Race is the central focus of this perspective, however, theorists recognize the intersectionality and fluidity of race, class, gender, sexual orientation, and other markers of difference. For this study, we were especially drawn to racial literacy because it strives to develop a set of social proficiencies that attempt to make sense of the discursive and performative systems of race and other identity markers (Bolgatz, 2005). Thus, to practice racial literacy, individuals engage in the following practices: (a) hear and appreciate diverse and unfamiliar experiences, (b) recognize how to ask questions, (c) view race as a structural rather than individual problem, (d) engage in talk even when it is difficult or awkward, (e) challenge undemocratic practices, (f) understand that racial identities are learned, and (g) facilitate problem-solving within the community (Guinier, 2004; Twine 2004). Consistently engaging in racial literacy requires practice and support, and can be done through structured dialogue. We used these seven elements along with the described four dimensions of critical literacy to better understand how teacher candidates engaged in analysis about how race, class, gender, and sexual orientation shaped how they positioned themselves and others. Specifically, we use the term critical conversations to include both elements of critical literacy and racial literacy.

Preservice Teachers' Critical Conversations

The study was conducted at a Southeastern university two years after the study we described in earlier chapters. Thus, participants were a new group of preservice English teachers (n=12) enrolled in the same seminar course described in earlier chapters who completed the same video analysis as described throughout the book. Because this follow up study focused specifically on how such analysis shaped students' discussion and reflection about the ways in which identity markers shaped teacher positionings, we examined the following data sources: (a) three audio-recorded small group conversations (30 minutes each); (b) two audio-recorded whole group conversations (total of one hour); and (c) 12 video assignments (video, reflection, and transcript). Table 6.1 indicates themes that were applied to the data to analyze the ensuing critical conversations.

Table 6.1 Characteristics of Critical Conversations

Characteristics of racism, classism, sexism, and heterosexism	Characteristics of critical conversations
Essentializing race, class, gender, or sexual orientation	Challenging undemocratic practices
Denying that race, class, gender, or sexual orientation matters (e.g., colorblindness)	Hearing and appreciating diverse or unfamiliar experiences and multiple perspectives
Viewing racism, feminism, classism, or heterosexism as outdated	Recognizing how to ask questions related to identity markers
Treating racism, feminism, classism, or heterosexism as extreme actions or words	Understanding that identities are learned
Considering racism, feminism, classism, or heterosexism as personal	Engaging in difficult and awkward talk
Regarding racism, feminism, classism, and heterosexism within the myth of individualism	Recognizing identities as a structural rather than individual problem
	Disrupting commonplace notions

Critical Conversations

We present three transcribed discussions (two whole group and one small group) to illustrate how our preservice teachers engaged in critical conversations about how their race, class, gender, and sexual orientation shaped teacher positionings. The first transcript explores how Amy and Mark modeled a critical conversation for the whole group. Next, we examine how the whole group engages in critical conversations about the ways in which gender and sexual orientation shape teacher positionings. The final scenario investigates a small group discussion about how race, class, and gender shape teacher identities. We end with this scenario because it illustrates how such critical conversations can shift preservice teachers' thinking about the impact of identity markers on practice.

Model Critical Conversation

As mentioned, we (Amy and Mark) video-recorded, transcribed, and analyzed a lesson from the English Methods course taught the previous semester. At the beginning of our two-hour seminar dedicated to discussing the video assignment, we wrote a series of questions on the board that included the following:

- How did you position yourself as a teacher?
- How did you position students as readers, writers, and/or participants?

- How were you positioned by your students?
- How did these positionings align (or not) with your desired teacher identities?
- In what ways does your race, class, gender, and sexual orientation shape your teacher positionings?

To begin, we showed the short clip to students and gave them the transcribed interaction. To model the kind of small group conversations we hoped the students would have, we sat at the front of the room and answered the questions we put on the board while students observed. Amy asked the questions and Mark answered them because he was the official instructor of that lesson. When we came upon the question regarding race, class, gender, and sexual orientation, the following discussion occurred:

> Mark: Well, in general, setting this particular segment aside, the fact that I'm White, male, and middle class is a position that I constantly have to work against in the sense that I live a privileged life in our society. And the assumptions I make as a teacher is not the reality for the kids I have in my classroom or the other adults in the learning situation—so the fact of being a male and being White is a challenge in that I question the assumptions I make at all times. In relation to the segment, when I do the kind of strategies that I employ in my classroom, they have to do with my students. That's also physically . . . so having a seat at the table for everyone is important. So positioning myself as someone in the background is important given my own race and gender and class. And so when I think of the segment these are the kind of things I want to see and take into consideration so I'm not making assumptions in ways that are marginalizing.
>
> Amy: Okay, so we practiced this earlier, and when I first asked Mark this question, he said: *I haven't thought about that!* And I'm not saying that to put him on the spot. I know you might also say *I haven't thought about that* or *it doesn't matter*. It does matter, so don't skip that question. Think about it because you know it's not always obvious. You know, these markers of difference shape who you are and how you talk to your students and the assumptions you make, so think about that. And like Mark said, he tried to put himself on the same level as his students and facilitate student voices so he is not the dominant voice.
>
> Mark: It's really difficult to articulate.
>
> Amy: And this really makes a difference, because we can accidentally be shutting a student down or excluding students by our behavior and not be aware of it. We all make those mistakes and it's good to recognize those occurrences.

> Mark: Speaking in a position of who I am, I just think that being a facilitator letting them speak and talk about without interrupting them is beneficial. Just getting different types of students the opportunity to speak . . .

In this conversation, Mark discussed two issues related to how his race, class, gender, and sexual orientation shaped his teaching within the transcript and in general. First, Mark stated that because he is a White, male, middle-class, and heterosexual teacher, he must question his assumptions about students. To reduce power hierarchies between students and the teacher, he takes two approaches illustrated in his video-recorded lesson. One of them is to physically be on the same level as students during discussions. He also attempts to foster multiple perspectives from students by asking various students to share their voices. Both specific examples illustrate how he enacts teacher identities that attempt to include, rather than exclude, students' backgrounds and experiences. Such analysis on his part models how to engage in difficult and awkward talk about his identity markers, and hear and appreciate diverse perspectives from his students. In addition, Mark's purposeful goals of inviting multiple perspectives and physically sitting with students illustrates his ability to promote social justice in his classroom by taking specific actions that attempt to level the field for students.

Another important point of this modeled critical conversation is the discussion about Mark's difficulty articulating how these markers of difference shaped the interactions in his video-recorded lesson. Many students have stated in the past that they also felt this way. By bringing this up, we attempted to help students understand that struggling with this question is the norm, rather than an indication that these markers of difference do not matter. Thus, the modeled critical conversation attempted to illustrate how to engage in difficult and awkward talk that recognized how identity markers shape teacher identities. By doing that, we hoped to open opportunities for students to explore, rather than dismiss, this topic. Below, we examine two transcripts in which students engage in small and whole group critical conversations to make sense of the ways in which markers of difference shape their teacher identities.

Gender and Sexual Orientation

The following conversation related to issues of gender and sexual orientation occurred during a whole group discussion after candidates discussed their video analysis projects in small groups. After asking candidates how race, class, gender, and sexual orientation shaped classroom interactions and positionings, Hillary stated that she noticed how her gender impacted the different ways she treated males and females in her classroom.

> Hillary: I feel like my gender kind of plays a role in how I interact with my male students. I noticed in the video that in first period

we were doing our warm up and everyone that was helping me were females and they were so eager to help and the only time I interacted with a male student is when I was telling him to put away a spoon. So I thought that was kind of pathetic. So that made me think, like, I wonder if it's because I'm a female. Or because a lot of it is because as a female it's like, you know, "Be careful, watch out." So, you know, I had my guard up ready for the worst comments ever and I never got a single one. Maybe like one time and that was it. So I felt like people kind of tricked me a little bit because I had this guard up but I didn't need to have the guard up really. And so in the future I'm going to work on building a relationship to them as much as I did with my females because I had more time to talk to them after class. But if a male stayed after class I didn't let it linger too much because it was like oh gosh what's he going to say. And so I think taking that time to build that relationship with all students regardless of gender is something I should work on in the future.

In this transcript, Hillary expressed her concern that she interacted more frequently and positively with female students. As she elaborated, she stated that this occurred often and she realized that it stemmed from a perceived necessity to distance herself from male students in order to maintain a professional relationship. Specifically, Hillary recognized that she was not treating her students equitably and through discussion she became aware that societal views played a part in how she positioned her male students. Later in the conversation, Hillary proposed a few ways for her to build relationships with her male students (e.g., talk to them in the hallway before class, make connections to their lives through planned lessons, stop only calling on males for behavior problems) while ensuring she sets clear boundaries for teacher/student relationships. Thus, Hillary recognizes that she can take action in this situation as a way of promoting social justice within her classroom. In addition, by making stronger connections with her male students, she will be better equipped to make curriculum changes in her ELA classroom that build on varying literacy and linguistic knowledge.

The critical conversation that followed Hillary's comment produced both a robust and fragile discussion about how gender shapes the ways in which teachers position themselves, their students, and how they are positioned by their students. After Hillary's statement, Mark asked the following:

Mark: Can I ask you a question? Who was saying be careful of the males?
Hillary: A lot of people, and a lot of my friends going into student teaching, especially in the high school levels, like parents and

Positions of Critical and Racial Literacy 103

people who had already student taught and teachers and some professors.

Mark: Okay, I wonder how this relates to how they position you—your parents, your teachers, your teacher friends—positioning you as a teacher? These are questions you have to consider. How does your OSTE [On-Site Teacher Educator] position you? It would be an interesting question to explore.

Hillary: My OSTE never really said anything like that. I don't think it's really a reflection of the people, more of like a reflection of society as a whole. It's up to the woman to protect herself against the comments that come in. . . . Like people talk about how women are on a rape schedule, where like you do certain things around the day to prevent anything bad from happening. For example, we walk swiftly to our cars and hold our keys out when we're walking at night we look like we are going somewhere so we're not targeted. So it's like up to us to protect ourselves instead of to people to stop being jerks and so I think that's the reason why females get told to watch out stems a lot from that.

Mark: Does anyone else have someone say watch out?

Grayson: On the opposite end of the spectrum there's a thing, all three of us [pointing to the males in the class] have had that experience or that advice given to us at some point in time. Like my OSTE recommends that when a female student stays after class, that I get the thing that we use to prop open the door and I prop open the door with it and position myself by the door so that any interaction we have can be readily overheard by other people.

Valerie: Why aren't we told to do that with the same gender? I feel like that if I am a female and there's a female student that it's just as important to have that door open.

Grayson: I feel that statistically it's just been more favored towards that [heterosexual relationships] and also questioning just the way the society works. There will be more questions if there was a female teacher with male students or male teacher with female student behind closed doors than there would be about other things.

Mark: . . . These are all questions we are all asking about how we position ourselves in relation to gender, and in some point sexual orientation.

From this transcript, we recognize the following ways in which preservice teachers engaged in critical conversations about how gender impacted both interactive and reflective positionings. First, Hillary stated that comments from friends, family, and professors shaped how she positioned herself as a female teacher and as a result impacted her interaction with males (i.e., being distant; focusing on negative behavior). She recognized, however, that those positionings are a result of how society views women in general (i.e., victims of sexual assault; responsible for safety). Discussing how societal factors shape identity constructions can be a powerful way for teacher candidates to make sense of their positionings and question positions that may not match up to their desired identities. For Hillary, her analysis of gender issues began with questions about her positionings in relation to male students (as seen in the opening transcript). Through written reflection and dialogue in small and large groups, Hillary recognized that the gender issues occurring in her local classroom were related to broader social and cultural issues that she would need to question in order to make changes for a more equitable classroom.

Second, Hillary questioned commonplace assumptions about the responsibility of females to protect themselves from males, rather than the responsibility of males to act respectfully toward women. Interestingly, Hillary relates this to her own positionings as a teacher and recognizes that until now, she had not questioned the commonplace assumptions about her role as a female teacher in relation to her male students. Instead, she took other people's advice without challenging it. Such questioning and connection to teaching experiences highlights Hillary's engagement in critical conversations.

The conversation became more fragile, however, when Valerie challenged undemocratic practices related to sexual orientation by asking the class why these positionings only related to male/female interactions. Grayson attempted to answer her by recognizing how society tends to focus only on heterosexual interactions. Again, this recognition of how social and cultural issues shape everyday interactions with students, particularly as it relates to gender and sexual orientation, opens room for identity work with these preservice teachers. At the same time, Grayson's comment appeared to diminish the significance of Valerie's point that society takes a heterosexist view of teacher/student relationships. As a result, that topic of conversation was not taken up. We view this as a missed opportunity for both instructors and students to ask more questions that disrupted these commonplace notions, challenged undemocratic practices, or shared experiences that might add new perspectives.

Race, Class, and Gender

Although gender was a constant thread throughout our class conversation, students in small groups also focused on the ways in which race and class shaped their teacher identities. In this small group conversation with Tammy and Emma, they shared five to ten minute clips of their teaching that coincided with their transcriptions and analysis. The following excerpt illustrates how they engaged in both a rich and fragile critical conversation about how identity markers impact teacher positionings.

Positions of Critical and Racial Literacy 105

Emma: Very nice, in what ways do race, gender, sexual orientation affect these interactions?

Tammy: Even on paper, I had a really hard time answering this question. I mean the school where I am, which is [SHS]. It's a very heavily African American community and that class in particular had more males but I just, I don't know. I don't honestly feel that I use my race or my gender to help in facilitating in their learning or anything. I don't see it like that. I just go in thinking that if they respect me, I respect them. If I respect them, they respect me. I mean maybe it does but I don't look at it as I'm an African American woman this is what I do. I project myself so they will respect me. They will see me as a facilitator or they will see me as a teacher. I really think it's how I present myself as a teacher as a facilitator, not as an African American female facilitator. Does that make sense?

Emma: Do you think it inhibits you in any way? Anything like that?

Tammy: I don't think so. I think it would in a different class? For instance, if I taught an IB [International Baccalaureate] class which is the exact opposite. There may be only two African Americans in that class. I think it would be a lot different if I taught that class and I kind of would not have a connection with them maybe because I never was in IB and I don't come from the same background as them maybe. In that sense it would maybe inhibit not facilitate their learning, but the connections could be made. Or maybe they would be able to see that I'm not comfortable or as like hip or up to speed about certain things that they are and actually I think if I would go there my race and everything would hinder me with my African American kids because I don't listen to rap music so when they talk to me about all these rappers and different issues I'm clueless, so I'm like tell me about it. So there is one kid. He called me bougie and you know that's acting uppity. I'm a Black girl and that's not me. That's how he perceived me. I don't think my race would hinder or facilitate the kids I have right now at this moment.

In this section, Tammy engaged in both rich and fragile moments within her critical conversations. First, Tammy admitted that this particular question was a challenge for her, because she did not see how her race or gender might facilitate or inhibit learning for students. Tammy appeared to take a colorblind approach by saying that her position as a facilitator is shaped by building respectful relationships, rather than her race. She related this to the fact that her classes are mostly African American students, implying that the similarity in backgrounds makes race matter less. At this point, Tammy took a colorblind approach by denying that race matters within this particular situation. She continued to engage in this critical conversation, however, by persisting with this topic.

Next, the critical conversation became more robust when Tammy shifted from a colorblind approach to the recognition that race might play a part in how she builds relationships with students. For instance, after Emma asked if these identity markers potentially inhibited her teacher identity enactments, Tammy explained that her race might make more of a difference if she were teaching a group of non-African American students. To be specific, she stated that she might not be able to connect with them because they did not share the same background and because she did not attend IB classes. Tammy also noted that sharing the same cultural background did not always make connections easy when she shared her example of students calling her uppity. Tammy's comments about attending IB and being called uppity related to issues of power and status most often associated with class. At this point, Tammy did not explicitly talk about issues of class and how they intersect with race; however, through her discussion she began to make evident the impact of identity markers on her teacher identity. Although she did not give specific evidence from her transcripts, she used hypothetical statements related to recent experiences to describe her shift in perspective. At this point, Tammy and Emma would benefit from another perspective from a classmate or questions that helped them disrupt commonplace assumptions about the complex ways in which both race and class impact teacher positioniongs.

Next, Emma (White, middle-class female) explored how her race, class, and gender shape her teacher positionings in a school with students from similar backgrounds.

> **Emma:** I am a White middle class female and that's fairly common in this school, but there's also a mixture of students that aren't as privileged as I am and they haven't lived the life I have lived. I have to remember not to exclude students that haven't been as privileged because there is a good mixture of students in school and I think just being female and kind of petite and young is difficult coming into the classroom so I have to position myself as an authority and in the video you really don't see that because by this point I feel that I made those boundaries clear. I came in very firm and this is what you have to do . . . so by this point the students knew that I mean business and that I'm okay with having fun as long as it doesn't cross the line with what is said. And I think that's very important being a young teacher coming in being authoritative and that you're in the position where you can give them consequences for their own actions.
> **Tammy:** That's really good. Can I add on to what you're saying?
> **Emma:** I'm done.

Tammy: In listening to what you're saying about race and gender, thinking back now on a lot of my kids' backgrounds, I know a lot of them come from broken homes or now they are in foster homes and such or they have an older sibling raising them or an aunt. Maybe they, so I think the reason why some of them are able to see me as a teacher is because as a Black female, maybe I fill in for that position. A maternal, I treat them as my kids, even though I'm not much older. I'm like the older sister, so maybe that's how I can use my race and gender to shape my interactions with my students.

Emma: Yeah, I think I have a couple students who are in foster care systems or have issues similar to that and I have a hard time dealing with them because I lived my privileged life and I have my mom and my dad. I try to approach that situation—is I look at it like a person has something they struggle with and I don't necessarily have to understand what you're going through to sympathize with you or empathize because I am a big proponent of not being a victim or telling our students you don't have to play the victim. You come from circumstances that are tough but you don't have to play the victim. I had stuff in my life too. I think that's important too when positioning yourself, regardless of your class race gender anything like that.

Right away, Emma engaged in critical conversations by recognizing that her status as a White, middle-class female helps her because she shares a similar background with her students. At the same time, she stated that her race and class inhibited her teacher identity positionings in relation to students who are less privileged than her, particularly if she unintentionally excludes them. In addition, Emma noted that not only her gender, but also her age and size shaped how she established authority in her cooperating teacher's classroom, a typical dilemma for young preservice teachers. By bringing up other identity markers (age and size), Emma broadened how instructors and candidates have been defining markers of difference. Thus, she shared another perspective that enriches the conversation. At this point, Emma did not seem to view this kind of discussion as difficult or awkward and this opened space for Tammy to build on her reflective thoughts, as discussed below.

Tammy's reflective response to Emma illustrated both critical and racial literacy and elements of oppressive talk. For example, Tammy added on by saying that Emma's points helped her to recognize how her gender and race might help her connect with students who view her as a maternal figure or older sister. This is another shift for Tammy, who previously stated that her race, class, gender, and sexual orientation did not impact her teaching.

The critical conversation turns fragile, however, when Tammy says that students viewed her as the maternal figure that many do not have. First, her comment illuminates the class divide between her and her students. By taking on the position of a maternal figure, she potentially situates herself as more privileged than her students. In addition, Tammy continued to use the statement, "How I can use my race and gender to shape my interactions . . ." Although it is true that she could use identity markers to actively shape interactions, she is still struggling to see that those identity markers act upon her no matter what. To enrich this critical conversation, other participants are needed to ask questions about the ways in which identities are structural and shape every situation. In addition, the conversation could have been more robust if another perspective was shared that discussed how the identities we bring to a classroom interaction may be predetermined by stereotypes or mainstream discourses about identity markers. Recognizing those occurrences can help preservice teachers be aware of changes they might need to make.

This transcript ends with Emma, who used language ("not being a victim") that illustrates some misconceptions about the ways in which social and cultural backgrounds shape a student's learning experience. Her statement is similar to a "pull yourself up by your bootstraps" approach that does not consider the realities of the barriers that students face. At this point, the critical conversation is fragile and in need of questions and perspectives that illuminate the ways in which various backgrounds impact the daily school lives of students. Tammy did engage the critical conversation by asking questions that challenged Emma's view. This might be a negative aspect of talking about these issues in pairs. Although the pairing might have fostered more trust between Tammy and Emma, a larger group might have provided more perspectives and challenging questions.

To conclude, we remind of you of the opening quote from Tammy, who ended our whole group conversation by admitting that she "had a really hard time answering the question about race, class, gender." She stated, however, that after listening to Emma, she thought more about identity markers and realized that "it really affects me in the classroom and my kids and their interactions." Her statement is significant because it illustrates how her engagement in critical conversations in both small and whole groups shifted how she viewed the ways in which identity markers impacted her teacher positionings. Although both Tammy and Emma still struggled to consistently take on critically and racially literate positions, this conversation suggests that students took on those positions more than they had in previous assignments in which they dismissed this question.

FINAL THOUGHTS

In an article about critical community building, Silvia Bettez (2011) acknowledged that as a teacher, it is important to her students that she "elicit their stories, acknowledge their ideas, and validate their experiences" (p. 3).

She recognized that one way to do that work as an instructor was through active listening that included asking critical questions, reflecting on what you might have learned, and being open to new ideas that differ from your worldviews. We mention this here to highlight the significance of modeling and practicing conversations that build community so that members can engage in dialogue about identity issues. In particular, this study illustrated how creating conversational guidelines, modeling dialogue, fostering discussion in small groups, and engaging in whole group conversation fostered critical perspective-taking in ways that a written reflection did not. We do believe, however, that following up with a written reflection after these discussions would help candidates think through and develop these understandings even more. Below, we discuss specific aspects of the discussions that facilitated or inhibited critical conversations and raise questions about more that can be done. We end with possible implications for teacher educators and researchers.

The modeled critical conversation appeared to facilitate critical conversations by illustrating how one might answer the question and by modeling how these discussions are not challenging just for preservice teachers, but also for experienced instructors. Such modeling of how a teacher uses specific evidence from a transcript to discuss how identity markers shape teaching played a part in moving some students from silence to engagement in critical conversations (Chavez-Reyes, 2012). As teacher educators, more questions were raised, however, about how to facilitate such conversations. For instance, what does a productive and helpful modeled critical conversation related to video analysis look like? How can teacher educators become better at articulating how our markers of difference shape our teacher identities? How can we help students identify their practices in the video that prompted reflections about how identity markers shaped teacher identities?

Another way that students engaged in critical conversations was by beginning with a topic that was most familiar or comfortable to them (gender). We noted this comfort by the frequency gender issues were brought up in this particular thread and throughout our seminar in general. We assume this may be because critical conversations about gender oppression are more normative and accepted, perhaps due to feminism being part of mainstream discourses historically longer than discussion about other identity markers, including racism or sexual orientation. Thus, candidates drew on personal experiences to discuss these issues (Depalma, 2010). In particular, preservice teachers discussed both local (e.g., Hillary's experience with male students) and global examples (e.g., the way society positions females as victims responsible for protecting themselves) related to how gender shapes teacher positionings (Mosley, 2010). The abilities to question commonplace assumptions and focus on sociopolitical issues are important tenets of critical conversations. In addition, we see that candidates recognize that these factors shape them, but that they also have some control in how they might shift teacher positionings to counteract oppressive acts. In other words, candidates positioned themselves as agents by facilitating problem solving within their classroom community (e.g., Hillary's suggestions for how to connect with her male students).

We also learned that students do not engage in all elements of critical conversations consistently. In other words, students engaged in a dialogue that positioned female students as predators and male and female teachers as victims. Although this might be the case in some instances, this duality between the two people does not promote complex thinking about these issues. Candidates also continued to dismiss certain identity markers. For example, Valerie brought up issues of heterosexism in the first transcript. This could have been an opportunity to engage in critical conversations about sexual orientation, but the topic was dismissed as something not relevant to their experience as teachers. As instructors, we wonder how to engage candidates in discussion about the identity markers which they feel the least comfortable discussing? What more could we have done to promote that complex thinking? What questions could we have asked to continue the critical conversation?

Finally, another aspect of critical conversations that appeared to shape engagement by participants was actively listening to instructors and small group partners. For Tammy, such active listening opened the opportunity for her to shift her thinking about these issues. Admittedly, she began by taking a colorblind approach to the question. At the end of the seminar, however, Tammy acknowledged that those identity markers did make a difference. Such a shift in thinking required her to listen to others in a nonjudgmental manner. From that, she critically reflected on the meaning of what she heard and as a result, her thought process changed. Although this shift in thinking is a move forward, Tammy's comment about being the mom that her students do not have raised questions for us. Such ways of thinking could lead to "othering" her students and creating a divide based on status. Although we recognize that Tammy does not intend for her thoughts to be taken this way, we wondered what questions we could ask to help Tammy continue to critically examine how her identity markers shape her teaching. Specifically, how could we foster more analysis about how that teacher identity might position students? These questions remind us that this kind of work is never complete. Thus, in a seminar course, how often should we engage in critical conversations? Will candidates continue to use such tools during their teaching career?

IT'S YOUR TURN: EXPLORING POSITIONS OF CRITICAL AND RACIAL LITERACY

We have included a few excerpts from candidates' written analyses in reference to the question about the ways in which race, class, gender, and sexual orientation shaped teacher identities. As someone learning the tenets of critical conversations discussed in this chapter, how might you respond to the following comments if they were stated in a small or large group setting? In what ways are they practicing critical and racial literacy (review Table 6.1 in the chapter for a reminder)? In what ways are they not?

Excerpt One (Bernard)

> I believe that as a Black male, I bring a certain kind of presence that demands respect because of the uncertainty of who I really am because I'm Black. Students are often guessing and trying to figure out my personality as well as my decision-making process. I keep them on their toes, so they never know what I'm going to do next. My resource class is all Black except three students in a class of 18. The Black students, especially the males, do not respect my OSTE who is White simply because he is White. I can give them a million assignments to do and they will do it or at least attempt it; whenever my OSTE has anything to say or wants to go over something with them, they tune out. They won't listen, and they say disrespectful things to him. I don't have that problem and I believe it is because I am a Black male which allows them to relate and identify with me.

From this excerpt, we understand that Bernard engaged in critical and racial literacy by openly discussing how his race shapes his teaching practices. Rather than deny that his identity as a Black male matters, Bernard used specific examples from his student teaching experience to illustrate his point ("I can give them a million assignments . . ."). With this example, he recognized that because his students share a cultural background similar to his own, they appeared to be more likely to "respect" him. At the same time, Bernard essentialized race by assuming that all Black students would respect him because he is Black and disrespect his OSTE because he is White. If Bernard shared this comment in a whole group discussion, we might ask him if there were any other reasons why students might not respect his OSTE. Or, we might ask him if he struggles to connect with students from other backgrounds and what he might do to gain respect from them. Finally, a critical conversation might benefit from another perspective that shares an experience about respecting teachers who come from different backgrounds than their own.

Excerpt Two (Milo)

> Race and gender don't play too much of a factor with me. They don't really feel one way or the other about my being half-Korean, as I've proved that I can relate to many different backgrounds. They may take me more seriously being a male rather than female, considering how often I see the male students flirting with the four female students in the classroom.

Milo's reflection attempted to explore how his identity markers impacted his teacher positionings by writing about the topic. His discussion, however, became fragile by stating that race and gender did not matter to him or his students because he has proven that he can relate to diverse backgrounds. To foster a critical conversation about this topic, we would ask Milo to talk about what he did to relate to his students with various backgrounds. In addition, multiple perspectives about how these connections must be continuously developed over time would enhance the critical conversation and possibly illuminate how issues of race and gender are never fully resolved. Such a question could open up concrete ways in which teachers develop relationships and connections with students from cultural and linguistic backgrounds different from their own. The second half of Milo's paragraph is also fragile, because he essentializes gender experiences by saying that he is taken more seriously as a male because male students flirt with females. To foster a critical conversation about gender issues, we would ask Milo about his link between males flirting with female students and respecting a male or female teacher.

After reading the robust and fragile examples of critical conversations, how might you change your interactional patterns to foster discussion about markers of difference? What kinds of questions can you ask? How would you pose those questions? What tone might you use? What sentence starters (e.g., I hear what you are saying) might you use when sharing a new perspective?

REFERENCES

Adler, S. M. (2011). Teacher epistemology and collective narratives: Interrogating teaching and diversity. *Teaching and Teacher Education, 27*(3), 609–618.

Baecher, L., & Kung, S. C. (2011). Jumpstarting novice teachers' ability to analyze classroom video: Affordances of an online workshop. *Journal of Digital Learning in Teacher Education, 28*(1), 16–26.

Betez, S. (2011). Critical community building: Beyond belonging. *Educational Foundations, 25*(3–4), 3–19.

Bolgatz, J. (2005). *Talking race in the classroom.* New York, NY: Teachers College Press.

Chavez-Reyes, C. (2012). Engaging in critical social dialogue with socially diverse undergraduate teacher candidates at a California State University. *Teacher Education Quarterly, 39*(2), 43–62.

Christensen, L. (2000). *Reading, writing, and rising up: Teaching about social justice and the power of the written word.* Milwaukee: Rethinking Schools.

Cruz-Janzen, M. I. (2000). From our readers: Preparing preservice teacher candidates for leadership in equity. *Equity & Excellence in Education, 33*(1), 94–101.

Daniel, B. (2009). Conversations on race in teacher education cohorts. *Teaching Education, 20*(2), 175–188.

DePalma, R. (2010). Toward a practice of polyphonic dialogue in multicultural teacher education. *Curriculum Inquiry, 40*(3), 436–453.

Fecho, B., Collier, N. D., Friese, E. E. G., & Wilson, A. (2010). Critical conversations: Tensions and opportunities of the dialogical classroom. *English Education, 42*(4), 427–447.

Frederick, R., Cave, A., & Perencevich, K. C. (2010). Teacher candidates' transformative thinking on issues of social justice. *Teaching and Teacher Education, 26*(2), 315–322.

Guinier, L. (2004). From racial liberalism to racial literacy: Brown v. Board and the interest divergence dilemma. *The Journal of American History, 91*(1), 92–118.

Janks, H. (2010). *Literacy and power.* New York: NY: Routledge.

Ladson-Billings, G. (1991). Beyond multicultural illiteracy. *Journal of Negro Education*, 60(2), 147–57.

Leland, C., Harste, J., Ociepka, A., Lewison, M., & Vasquez, V. (1999). Exploring critical literacy: You can hear a pin drop. *Language Arts*, 77(1), 70–77.

Lewison, M., Flint, A. S., & Van Sluys, K. (2002). Taking on critical literacy: The journey of newcomers and novices. *Language Arts*, 79(5), 382–392.

MacPherson, S. (2010). Teachers' collaborative conversations about culture: Negotiating decision making in intercultural teaching. *Journal of Teacher Education*, 61(3), 271–286.

McIntyre, A. (1997). *Making meaning of Whiteness: Exploring racial identity with White teachers*. Albany, NY: State University of New York Press.

McLaren, P. (1998). *Life in schools. An introduction to critical pedagogy in the foundations of education*. New York: Pearson.

Milner, H. R. (2006). Preservice teachers' learning about cultural and racial diversity: Implications for urban education. *Urban Education*, 41(4), 343–375.

Mosley, M. (2010). Becoming a literacy teacher: Approximations in critical literacy teaching. *Teaching Education*, 21(4), 403–426.

Parker, B., & Howard, A. (2009). Beyond economics: Using social class life-based literary narratives with pre-service and practicing social studies and English teachers. *High School Journal*, 92(3), 3–13.

Pewewardy, C. (2005). Shared journaling: A methodology for engaging White preservice students into multicultural education discourse. *Teacher Education Quarterly*, 32(1), 41–60.

Rogers, R., & Christian, J. (2007). 'What could I say?': A critical discourse analysis of the construction of race in children's literature. *Race Ethnicity and Education*, 10(1), 21–46.

Schieble, M. (2012a). A critical discourse analysis of teachers' views on LGBT literature. *Discourse: Studies in the Cultural Politics of Education*, 33(2), 207–222.

Schieble, M. (2012b). Critical conversations on whiteness with young adult literature. *Journal of Adolescent and Adult Literacy*, 56(3), 212–221.

Sherin, M. G., & van Es, E. (2009). Effects of video club participation on teacher's professional vision. *Journal of Teacher Education*, 60(1), 20–37.

Sleeter, C. E. (2008). Critical family history, identity, and historical memory. *Educational Studies*, 43(2), 114–124.

Sleeter, C.E. (2011). Becoming White: Reinterpreting a family story by putting race back into the picture. *Race, Ethnicity, and Education*, 14(4), 421–433.

Sleeter, C. E., Torres, M.N., & Laughlin, P. (2004). Scaffolding conscientization through inquiry in teacher education. *Teacher Education Quarterly*, 31(1), 81–96.

Smith, K. (2001). Critical conversations in difficult times. *English Education*, 33(2), 153–165.

Skerrett, A. (2011). English teachers' racial literacy knowledge and practice. *Race, Ethnicity and Education*, 14(3), 313–330.

Twine, F. W. (2004). A White side of Black Britain: The concept of racial literacy. *Ethnic and racial studies*, 27(6), 878–907.

Vetter, A., Meacham, M., & Schieble, M. (2013). Leveling the field: Negotiating positions of power as a preservice teacher. *Action in Teacher Education*, 35(4), 230–251.

Zeichner, K.M., & National Center for Research on Teacher Learning. (1993). *Educating teachers for cultural diversity*. NCRTL Special Report. Retrieved November 21, 2014, from http://ncrtl.msu.edu/http/sreports/sr293.pdf

7 Implications for Identity Work and Video Analysis in Teacher Education

EXPLORING IDENTITY WORK IN TEACHER EDUCATION

> Telling teachers to increase collaboration in their classrooms is not sufficient. . . . To be able to act productively to change the situation, we need to understand how to see the worlds in which we and our students have invested identities and the assumptions guiding the discursive choices we have available to us.
>
> Rex & Schiller, 2009, p. 43

We begin with this quote to illustrate the importance of providing structured opportunities for preservice teachers to engage in identity work through video analysis. Without data of classroom interactions through modes including video, preservice teachers rely on memory and their construction of events to engage in reflection of teaching and learning (Rosaen, Lundeberg, Cooper, Fritzen, & Terpstra, 2008). The chapters in this book portray specific discourse analytic approaches using positioning theory that open opportunities for candidates to focus on how their linguistic and nonverbal choices impact the enactment of identities related to teaching and learning. This type of framework helps candidates notice how they build relationships with students and scaffold academic language in ways that invite students to see themselves as capable literacy learners and take more ownership over their learning. In other words, this approach opens opportunities for candidates to consider how particulars of practice are broken down for the purpose of learning more about certain aspects of teaching (e.g., decomposing practice) (Grossman et al., 2009). As a result, preservice teachers are able to see and enact elements of practice more effectively. Below, we discuss what we, as teacher educators, learned from our students' analytic process. Specifically, we discuss how such analysis revealed alignments and misalignments in teacher identity work, highlighted a need to focus on interactive positionings related to the ELA content area, and illuminated the benefits of considering student perspectives.

Alignments and misalignments in teacher identity work. As preservice teachers in this book highlighted, discourse analysis of transcribed video-recorded interactions illustrated how they positioned themselves as teachers during moment-to-moment interactions. Such illustrations became especially important when teacher candidates examined how those positionings both aligned and misaligned with desired teacher identities for various reasons. For example, Erica's desired identities as an advocate aligned with moment-to-moment positionings in her work with an individual student. This contrasted with Jay, whose positionings misaligned with his preferred identities of a power-share critical pedagogy teacher. In addition, Jaina struggled to define what she meant by a facilitator identity, which shaped how she enacted that identity over time. We believe that the analysis of transcribed interactions was key in helping these candidates decompose their practice because such micro-analysis required that they slow down their examinations (Sherin & Van Es, 2009) and provide evidence for claims they made about reflexive and interactive positionings. Thus, such analysis helped them to think deeply about how to put their teacher philosophies into practice (Overbaugh, 1995).

As the preservice teachers expressed in their reflections, the analysis prompted reflection about how alignments and misalignments occurred because of both micro- and macro-factors (e.g., classroom or societal issues). For example, Erica was able to align her identities with support from her cooperating teacher. Jay, however, was not able to align his desired identities with practice because his students did not yet trust him as a teacher. Such trust was related to differing cultural and linguistic backgrounds. For Hillary, the analysis revealed how gender issues constituted a broad social and cultural factor that shaped her micro-interactions with students. With this awareness, she was able to develop a plan of action that changed some of her behaviors. Such plans illustrate candidates' abilities to be agents of change in their classroom and schools. Without those acts of agency, the above identity work might seem pointless. Preservice teachers, however, need support as they explore alignments and misalignments (Alsup, 2006). Teacher educators can provide that support during teacher education courses. Below we have a few suggestions for how to do that.

Implications for practice. Rather than dive right into discourse analysis, we have found it to be helpful to engage students in identity work in various ways and throughout multiple courses. For example, to prepare preservice teachers to analyze both alignments and misalignments, we first asked them to create a teacher philosophy statement, as described in chapter one, that they put on a teacher website. Candidates returned to this philosophy as they engaged in discourse analysis about the video-recorded lessons to examine if their enactments align or misalign with their preferred teacher identities. Because students have written this kind of philosophy in other courses, Amy found it helpful to ask students to write a series of *This I Believe* statements. Such statements were drawn from the popular *This I Believe* essays featured on National Public Radio (http://thisibelieve.org/) that showcase written commentary about a variety of topics, such as family or democracy. By modifying their philosophy into brief statements, preservice teachers create concise bullet points that they can turn into practice over their yearlong fieldwork. In addition, a list of beliefs is more likely to draw the attention of students, parents, and colleagues who briefly visit the website. Below, we have included an example from a student teacher:

This I believe . . .

I am the mediator in the classroom. I want my students to take the knowledge from my hands and run away with it. I want them to realize that they were born leaders. Some can talk, others can listen, but all of them can learn from one another.

I believe everything is connected—history, politics, sociology, pop culture. The connection is life.

I believe in . . .

- Discussion
- Discipline
- Intrigue
- Knowledge is not fixed
- Preparing my students to ask *and* answer the tough questions

I want to be a teacher who is humble. Who knows that I will make mistakes and hope my students realize that I am human. I want to have a classroom with consistency and managed time. There must be organization for everything planned and flexibility if those plans fall through. Respect must be at the forefront of this classroom.

By having this document, preservice teachers are able to return to their statements and examine evidence about how they hope to position themselves. To help preservice teachers engage in a rich examination, teacher educators can ask candidates to decompose those philosophical positionings and think about how they will put that plan into practice. For instance, if a candidate says they want to be an organized and flexible teacher, then what does that mean? What does that look like? Finally, as mentioned previously, these philosophical statements provide a place for students to engage in robust analysis about identity alignments and misalignments based on evidence rather than memory.

Need to focus on interactive positionings related to the ELA content area. We believe it is beneficial for preservice teachers to examine how the language they use can both include and exclude students as members of the classroom community (Rex & Schiller, 2009). Engagement and participation are certainly one aspect of that examination. For example, Erica wrote about a time when she shut down a student comment about a poem they read in order to move on to test practice. She recognized that this interactional choice positioned her students as non-participants in the classrooms. Thus, through her word choice, she inadvertently told students that their personal interest in a poem was not valued in the class, even though we know she did value this work. What was valued based on macro-level pressures, however, was test practice. Although this conflicted with her preferred goals of advocating for students and integrating relevant material into the curriculum, she recognized that institutional constraints and pressures impact the choices teachers make. For Erica, this analysis opened a space for her to be aware of students' identities as learners and reflect on how their response to specific interactions shape learning. Thus, the analysis of how a teacher positions students during interactions can uncover how and why students adopt particular identities over time (e.g., comedian or resistant student) so that teachers can make interactional shifts that open up new ways of positioning from students (Vetter, Meacham, & Schieble 2013). What is missing, however, is a structured analysis of how these interactions position students as readers and writers. Because we believe that ELA teaching involves fostering the reading and writing identities of students, how might we support preservice teachers to think more about how to do this? We provide one suggestion below.

Implications for practice. One way to have preservice teachers think about fostering the reader/writer identities of students in their ELA classrooms is to ask them to think about what those identities mean to them. For instance, Amy asks her candidates to complete the following sentences: A writer is . . . A reader is . . . To get them thinking, she provides a few quotes from writers:

> You see, in my view a writer is a writer not because she writes well and easily, because she has amazing talent, because everything she does is golden. In my view a writer is a writer because even when there is no hope, even when nothing you do shows any sign of promise, you keep writing anyway.—Junot Diaz
>
> And by the way, everything in life is writable about if you have the outgoing guts to do it, and the imagination to improvise. The worst enemy to creativity is self-doubt.—Sylvia Plath
>
> The more that you read, the more things you will know. The more that you learn, the more places you'll go.- Dr. Seuss, *I Can Read With My Eyes Shut!*

In response to this assignment, preservice teachers have written the following:

> *The life of a writer is much like that of an explorer, or archeologist. Always looking, always digging for new thoughts, new ways of thinking, in hopes of coming one step closer to the truth.*
> *Readers search outside themselves to find themselves.*

> Reading is the way we share a corner of our minds with the thoughts of others, the ways we absorb the world, explore the world, and change the world.

After preservice teachers write their statements, they create a visual (paper or digital) to illustrate what they have written. After they have both a visual and a written statement, candidates share them as a class. This exercise helps future literacy teachers think about how they intend to situate their students in their classroom. If, in their analysis, they can return to statements about how they hope to position their students, then they can be more purposeful about analyzing how they position their students as readers and writers and resist specific positionings that do not align with their beliefs. In other words, they can critically examine if they are situating students as test writers when they hoped to integrate more creative writing into their classroom. We believe that this kind of work shifts the focus from reflective positioning about teacher identities to more specific interactive positionings about the reader/writer identities of ELA students. Similar to what one candidate wrote in his reflection in regards to how he positioned students, he realized that he needed to focus less on himself and encourage "students to pursue their own lines of thought." Sometimes, however, students' "own lines of thought" are silenced with pressures to write in ways that are valued by the district or state (e.g., short answers; five-paragraph essays). Through exercises like the one mentioned above, teacher educators can foster more dialogue about how to negotiate pressures from outside the classroom with pedagogical beliefs about teaching literacy.

Benefits of considering students' perspectives. The preservice teachers in this book also had the chance to decompose practice about how students positioned them as teachers. As Harper mentioned in chapter one, it is valuable to think about students' perspectives—"from the other side of the desk." For example, Erica was able to see that her students also situated her as an advocate by telling her so. This interaction validated that students recognized her as the kind of teacher she hoped to be. In contrast, Jaina noted that students situated her as the holder of all knowledge as opposed to a facilitator of student thought. This contradiction indicated that Jaina might need to behave in different ways before students recognized her as the facilitator she hoped to be. It is difficult, however, to know for sure how students position teachers, so candidates must seek it out. We have a few practical suggestions for ways to foster such analysis in a teacher education course.

Implications for practice. To decompose practice related to student perspectives, we found it helpful to interview students about how they view teacher candidates. For us, we made the interviews an option for students' third video for their analysis project. Below, we provide a few excerpts from a written reflection by Kayla, who recorded the responses of her students after asking them what they thought of her teaching so far.

Many of my students found my strong suit to be that I got to know the students individually. I struggled the first few weeks to know everyone's names in my classes, but by the end of my third week I could go around naming each student, along with their favorite band, the sports they play, and the areas that they excelled and struggled at in school. This video showed me how much students notice and respond to a teacher's ability to care about them. Additionally, my students liked that I did not give up on them. . . . K was one of my students that chose to give me the hardest time. . . . Luckily, I constantly chose to talk with him about his grades, work ethic, and behavior. . . . K expressed how he thought one of my best teaching qualities was that I stayed on him and made him do his work. I believe having one of my most difficult students tell me that was one of the best pieces of validation I could have received.

I believe these videos show my students positioning me as a teacher that they ultimately respected and learned from. I have also found that my pedagogy from last semester has drastically changed since the completion of my student teaching. My educational philosophy centered on just that—philosophy. Being in a classroom five days a week with 30 students at a time has given me a much more realistic and helpful approach to teaching. I have realized that I am helping to shape future community members, not merely generic cohorts of students. My pedagogy is now more focused on producing lessons that encourage my students to develop into honest and productive community members.

For Kayla, the interview with students validated her work with students, specifically in relation to knowing the lives of her students and being persistent with resistant students. At the end of her reflection, she noted that her theories of teaching have now turned into her practice. As a result, her teaching philosophy has shifted to focus more on helping students become productive community members. This third video, then, opened up opportunities to learn about how students positioned her as a teacher. Consequently she negotiated some of her desired teacher positionings to fit the needs of her students.

Overall, we found that this analysis project opened opportunities for preservice teachers to slow down analysis, to examine how to put their teacher philosophies into practice, and to improve instruction. In addition, the focus on discourse analysis and identity work helped candidates utilize evidence from transcripts to examine alignments and misalignments in desired teacher identities and explore ways to negotiate teacher identities within various school contexts.

TROUBLESHOOTING IDENTITY WORK IN TEACHER EDUCATION

Discourse analysis is tedious and difficult work. Transcribing and analyzing video-recorded interactions is tedious and difficult work, especially when novice teachers are still learning how to create lessons and manage students. In particular, this assignment challenges students to think critically about both interactive and reflective positionings related to the language they use. Most likely, these are new ways of thinking for student teachers and their first attempts will be surface-level. Over the years, we have found the following instructional strategies to be helpful:

- Engage in discourse analysis with candidates based on a video from a general teaching website, such as *Teaching Channel*. This is a great place to start. The analysis is not personal and it gives preservice teachers a chance to practice critical conversations around a specific classroom interaction.
- Ask candidates to read and discuss articles or chapters about teacher positionings and identity work.
    - Any chapter from *Choice Words: How Our Language Affects Children's Learning* by Peter Johnston
    - Any chapter from *Using Discourse Analysis to Improve Classroom Interaction* by Lesley Rex and Laura Schiller
    - "Positioning Students as Readers and Writers: An Examination of Teacher's Improvised Responses in a High School English Classroom" by Amy Vetter in *English Education*
- Model critical conversations for candidates using instructor's transcripts and analysis.
- Instructors should also record, transcribe, and analyze teaching. Not only is it beneficial for candidates to engage in critical conversations using the instructor's transcripts and analysis as a model, it is also productive for instructors to engage in this kind of analysis to recognize areas in which stereotypes are reinforced or critical opportunities for discussion are missed.
- Create guidelines for talking about these issues. The following resources might be helpful:
    - "Critical Community Building: Beyond Belonging" by Silvia Bettez in *Educational Foundations*
    - *Talking Race in the Classroom* by Jane Bolgatz
    - "Engaging in Critical Social Dialogue with Socially Diverse Undergraduate Teacher Candidates at a California State University" by Christina Chavez-Reyes in *Teacher Education Quarterly*
- Provide time in small groups to discuss.
- Provide time to debrief in whole groups.
- After in-class discussions, provide time for candidates to record what they learned and take note of any specific changes they plan to make for the rest of their student teaching.
- Promote discussion and practice about how to foster critical conversations in ELA classrooms. The following resources would be helpful:
    - "Critical Conversations: Tensions and Opportunities of the Dialogical Classroom" by B. Fecho, N.D. Collier, E.E.G. Friese, & A. Wilson in *English Education*

- "Critical Conversations on Whiteness with Young Adult Literature" by Melissa Schieble in the *Journal of Adolescent and Adult Literacy*
- "Moving Beyond the Inclusion of LGBT-Themed Literature in English Language Arts Classrooms: Interrogating Heteronormativity and Exploring Intersectionality" by M. Blackburn and J.M. Smith in the *Journal of Adolescent & Adult Literacy*.

Students may resist intensive and structured reflective work. Student teaching is typically the most challenging experience for our preservice teachers. They are expected to take on all duties of their cooperating teacher and fulfill university expectations. Intensive and structured reflection, such as the video analysis assignment, can seem like an overwhelming task as they prepare for lessons, reread literature, and manage students. To be specific, a few candidates wrote in their final reflection that they did not find the structured reflections to be beneficial. For instance, Andy wrote the following:

> I believe that every teacher at every step should constantly reflect on their practice. I do not believe that the video project helped me in this area . . . I feel I reflect a great deal already. I find that I need a way to turn off the instant-replay section of my brain. *Should I have worded my answer to Brenda Daniels differently? Did I silence my students when I referenced a question as being easy?*

Andy's perspective shows that the assignment might make it hard for candidates who are already reflecting about the ways in which their language shapes their teaching to turn off their thoughts about teaching when a break is needed. Perhaps for Andy, adding more in-depth reflection provoked more anxiety than constructive problem-solving. Thus, for those students who experience anxiety from this kind of reflection, it would help to focus on creating plans of action. That way the analysis becomes something concrete and tangible that can be solved in the future.

Another student, Diego, stated:

> Overall, I believe that the video analysis has helped me learn a lot about my teaching by allowing me to see things that you cannot see while teaching. I do not see, however, the need to write my thoughts out into paragraphs for what I have already mentally decided to do. I think that watching the video was far more beneficial than writing out what I thought about the video and how to adjust. I would prefer just making notes. I feel like it's tedious and unnecessary towards my progression.

For Diego, a written reflection made the analysis more tedious and he believed that he could have benefitted in the same way by watching the video and taking notes. To modify for classes, especially if time is a factor, students could engage in an informal written analysis in class, rather than at home.

This would be helpful to do before and after small and whole group conversations with their peers.

We include this commentary here to illustrate some of the constructive criticism you might receive for asking students to engage in this kind of analysis. Despite their suggestions, they also admitted they plan to use some form of it in the future. For example, Andy said:

> Due to this project, I asked my students to annotate audio recordings of their fishbowls. I saw a substantial improvement, and a ton of complaints, after their first transcription.

In addition, Diego stated:

> That being said, I really did benefit from the transcription part in the first video. Although I hated doing it, it was great to actually slow the classroom experience down into understandable language to really see what is actually going on. Overall, I think that the video recording is an amazing tool and I plan to continue doing it throughout my teaching experience to allow me to get a better perspective of how my students are learning in the classroom.

Overall, we think that it is important to ask for feedback from teacher candidates and modify the assignment to fit those needs. Three videos during one semester may prove to be too much for teacher candidates who also have several other requirements to fulfill during their student teaching. Focusing on the quality of one video analysis rather than the quantity of three might promote more in-depth analysis and allow teacher educators to provide the support that preserive teachers need.

Schools may be hesitant to allow student teachers to video record in the classroom. Every district and school will have a different policy regarding video recording in the classroom. For Amy, several teachers in her district sought certification by the National Board for Professional Teaching Standards. This certification involves several video-recorded lessons along with reflective analysis. As a result, most public high schools have students and parents/guardians sign a video permission form upon entering the ninth-grade. Teacher candidates can access that form through the administration to learn which students are not allowed to be recorded. In addition, Amy's student teachers send a letter home explaining the video analysis project. Parents/guardians only sign and return it if they prefer for their child *not* to be recorded. If preservice or cooperating teachers have a website, the letter could also be posted there for easy access. Preservice teachers situate the camera so that it does not record students who prefer not to be on video and none of the videos are made public. Below, we include a checklist for video recording in K–12 schools and an example parental permission form.

CHECKLIST FOR VIDEO RECORDING IN K–12 SCHOOLS

School Permission

    ____ Gain permission from classroom teacher to video record students
    ____ Contact principal to gain permission to video record students
    ____ Consult with classroom teacher about distributing forms
    ____ Distribute Parental Permission Form to every student in the class
    ____ Collect signed Parental Permission Form from students who do not want to be recorded
    ____ Copy signed forms and give one set to your cooperating teacher

PARENTAL PERMISSION FORM

Dear Families,

I am completing an assignment for my undergraduate course in Student Teaching for English Education. Part of this assignment involves video recording several lessons that I teach throughout the semester. The purpose of these recordings is to analyze and improve my teaching practices. Although your child is not the focus of these video recordings, I am writing to request your permission to video record in their classroom. The videos will not be posted publicly, nor will I identify your child by his/her full name when discussing the assignment with classmates and instructors.

Thank you,

PUT YOUR NAME HERE

SIGNATURE HERE

    I DO NOT give consent for video recordings of my child.

    Parent/Guardian Signature   Date

Teachers may experience technical difficulties. One of the most significant challenges with video analysis relates to the technology required to carry out this work. What kinds of cameras should students use? How do they submit their videos to their instructor or to each other for viewing? What are the optimal conditions for video recording? We have found flexibility and practice to be the most important points of consideration for dealing with issues related to video recording. For example, Melissa allows her candidates to record their teaching using a device of their choice. In addition to the standard video cameras available at her institution for borrowing, students also may use their own iPads and iPhones, which are beneficial because many novice teachers have continued to record their practice when they realize they can use their own personal devices. Often, the size of the video file becomes an issue when teacher candidates try to share their videos with others, however, so Melissa always recommends that they practice video recording a lesson first and try out a few different platforms for sharing video files. Google Drive and Vimeo are two free, password protected web-based platforms for sharing video that Melissa uses in her seminar. Melissa's institution has developed a video library for sharing videos that is useful, but requires significant infrastructure and investment that may not be possible. To address issues with a viable platform for video analysis, web-based portfolio systems such as Digication have been explored at Melissa's institution. The benefit of using a platform such as Digication is that the technology is consistently updated for a fee that colleges and universities can pay without the cost or responsibility for maintaining their own systems.

For further information regarding technological issues related to video analysis and additional ways of thinking about the role of video recording, annotation tools, and video clubs for teacher preparation, we recommend the following resources:

- *Digital Video for Teacher Education* edited by Brendan Calandra and Peter J. Rich, published by Routledge
- "Video Annotation Tools: Technologies to Scaffold, Structure, and Transform Teacher Reflection" by Peter Rich and Michael Hannafin in *Journal of Teacher Education*
- "How Different Video Club Designs Support Teachers in 'Learning to Notice'" by Elizabeth van Es and Miriam Gamoran Sherin in *Journal of Computing in Teacher Education*
- "Five Research-based Heuristics for Using Video in Pre-Service Teacher Education" by Geraldine Blomberg et al. in *Journal for Educational Research Online*

Your course includes inservice teachers, K–12 teachers, or teachers in various content areas. The set of questions we developed for the assignment could be useful for candidates across all content areas, grade levels, and contexts because they ask questions that speak to the development of teachers in general. Teacher educators could modify some of the questions to fit specific levels or areas, such as: How do you position your students as historians, mathematicians, or scientists? Additional questions might focus on helping inservice teachers recognize how micro- and macro- factors impact their identity work and might include: How do school policies or your cooperating teacher's expectations shape the way you position yourself and your students? Do these factors help or hinder your work to enact your desired teacher identities?

Final Thoughts

In Janet Alsup's (2006) book, *Teacher Identity Discourses*, she complicates the notion of identity from understanding it as a development of professional demeanor or dress to issues related to the "integration of personal self with the professional self, and the 'taking on' of a culturally scripted, often narrowly defined, professional role while maintaining individuality" (p. 4). She recognizes that fostering such discussions about professional identity work in teacher education courses is difficult and might expose some of our (teacher educators) own perceived weaknesses. With that in mind, we hope this book has provided some practical ways in which teacher educators can engage preservice teachers in that difficult work. Overall, we are confident that our students engaged in identity work that allowed them the opportunity to reflect on how they constructed and enacted teacher identities within moment-to-moment interactions and over time. Students engaged in conversations about alignments and misalignments related to desired identities and reflected about how teacher identities shape the world around them, including the agency to effect change. More research, however, could be done to provide more support for teacher educators and preservice teachers. To conclude, we provide a few suggestions below.

The use of discourse analysis with video in teacher education to foster identity work or teacher development in general is a growing area for researchers. For future research in this area, we suggest the following avenues. First, as literacy teacher educators, we see value in learning more about how discourse analysis with video might help teachers take on the identity of literacy teachers (e.g., writing workshop teacher) or situate students as readers and writers. Such research could combine content with pedagogical knowledge within an identity framework. This work would also help bridge the substantive research we have in literacy education on identity with practice. This process takes conversations about identity toward an applied construct for noticing, tracking, and improving teaching and learning, not just a theoretical construct that many new teachers find disconnected from the work of classroom teachers. In other words, more research that extends the notion that talk is a central tool to teaching is needed. As Johnston (2004) stated in *Choice Words*, "Teachers play a critical role in arranging the discursive histories from which these children speak.... With it they mediate children's activity and experience, and help them make sense of learning, literacy, life and themselves" (2004, p. 4). More research that helps teachers investigate how their talk fosters and hinders learning is needed in various contexts.

Second, we suggest more research about fostering critical conversations through discourse analysis. Specifically, educators would benefit from more qualitative research studies that illustrate how specific strategies, such as modeled critical conversations or open-ended questions, foster or constrain critical conversations within various contexts with diverse participants over time. Third, we believe that teacher educators would benefit from research that investigates how the examination of particular desired identities might foster a more robust understanding of identity construction and enactment. For instance, if a student teacher says they want to take on a culturally responsive teacher identity, it would seem that the candidate would first need to know what that means. What behaviors are associated with that identity and how might a teacher enact such identities within various kinds of contexts? How can we help preservice teachers prepare for that work?

REFERENCES

Alsup, J. (2006). *Teacher identity discourses: Negotiating personal and professional spaces*. Mahwah, NJ: Lawrence Erlbaum.

Bettez, S. (2011). Critical community building: Beyond belonging. *Educational Foundations, 25*(3–4), 3–19.

Blackburn, M. V., & Smith, J. (2010). Moving beyond the inclusion of LGBT-themed literature in English language arts classrooms: Interrogating heteronormativity and exploring intersectionality. *Journal of Adolescent and Adult Literacy, 53*(8), 625–634.

Blomberg, G., Renkl, A., Sherin, M. G., Borko, H., & Seidel, T. (2013). Five research-based heuristics for using video in preservice teacher education. *Journal for Educational Research Online, 5*(1), 3–33.

Bolgatz, J. (2005). *Talking race in the classroom*. New York, NY: Teachers College Press.

Calandra, B., & Rich, P. J. (Eds.). *Digital video for teacher education: Research and practice* New York, NY: Routledge.

Chavez-Reyes, C. (2012). Engaging in critical social dialogue with socially diverse undergraduate teacher candidates at a California State University. *Teacher Education Quarterly, 39*(2), 43–62.

Fecho, B., Collier, N. D., Friese, E. E. G., & Wilson, A. (2010). Critical conversations: Tensions and opportunities of the dialogical classroom. *English Education, 42*(4), 427–447.

Grossman, P., Compton, C., Igra, D., Ronfeldt, M., Shahan, E., & Williamson, P. W. (2009). Teaching practice: A cross-professional perspective. *Teachers College Record, 111*(9), 2055–2100.

Johnston, P. (2004). *Choice words: How our language affects children's learning*. Portland, ME: Stenhouse.

Overbaugh, R. C. (1995). The efficacy of interactive video for teaching basic classroom management skills to pre-service teachers. *Computers in Human Behavior, 11*(3–4), 511–527.

Rex, L., & Schiller, L. (2009). *Using discourse analysis to improve classroom interaction*. New York, NY: Routledge.

Rich, P. J., & Hannifin, M. (2009). Video annotation tools: Technologies to scaffold, structure, and transform teacher reflection. *Journal of Teacher Education, 60*(1), 52–67.

Rosaen, C., Lundeberg, M., Cooper, M., Fritzen, A., & Terpstra, M. (2008). Noticing noticing: How does investigation of video records change how teachers reflect on their experiences? *Journal of Teacher Education, 59*(4), 347–360.

Schieble, M. (2012b). Critical conversations on whiteness with young adult literature. *Journal of Adolescent and Adult Literacy, 56*(3), 212–221.

Sherin, M. G., & van Es, E. (2009). Effects of video club participation on teacher's professional vision. *Journal of Teacher Education, 60*(1), 20–37.

van Es, E., & Sherin, M. G. (2006). How different video club designs support teachers in "learning to notice." *Journal of Computing in Teacher Education, 22*(4), 125–135.

Vetter, A. (2010). Positioning students as readers and writers: An examination of teacher's improvised responses in a high school English classroom. *English Education, 43*(1), 33–64.

Vetter, A., Meacham, M., & Schieble, M. (2013). Leveling the field: Negotiating positions of power as a preservice teacher. *Action in Teacher Education, 35*(4), 230–251.

Appendix A
Video Analysis Assignment

Make sure to upload a five to ten minute segment of your video-recorded lesson to YouTube with a private link. That link will be shared with members of your small group and turned in with your final assignment. You can gain access to video cameras from the university library, Teaching Resource Center, and the media center at your school. Start early in case you have technical difficulties. Be ready to share in small groups on the seminar days specified in the syllabus.

Video One

- Videotape an entire lesson of you facilitating learning in direct or indirect instruction. This can include a lecture, mini-lesson, discussion, and/or reading instruction.
- Transcribe 5–10 minutes of instruction, including both teacher and student talk.
- In a 2–3 page analysis, answer the following questions:
  - Who does the most talking?
  - What kinds of questions are posed? What kinds of answers are facilitated?
  - How do you talk to students? What is your tone? Do you use directives? Questions? Praises? Criticisms?
  - How do you think your words positioned your students as readers and writers? How do you think your students positioned you as a teacher? How did you position yourself as a teacher?
  - How might these positionings be shaped by how you were taught? By the kind of school you attended? By your race, class, gender, and/or sexuality?
  - What are the strengths? What will you do differently?
  - How did these positionings align (or not) with your desired teacher identities?

Video Two

- Videotape your students while you facilitate instruction. This could be a lecture, mini-lesson, discussion, reading instruction, writing workshop, and/or small group work.
- Write a summary of what you see, including both verbal and nonverbal behavior. Some of this description can include short transcripts.

(*Continued*)

- In a 2–3 page analysis, answer the following questions:
  - What are students doing?
  - Are they engaged in the lesson?
  - How do they communicate with each other?
  - How do they position each other as readers and writers?
  - How do they position you as a teacher?
  - What are the strengths? What will you do differently?

Video Three

- Videotape a lesson of your choice. Think about an area in which you struggle and analyze your video based on that area. For example, you might write an analysis of your classroom management skills, how you facilitate discussion, or engage students in a mini-lesson. You might also interview students and request feedback about your teaching. Such information could help you learn more about how students position you as a teacher.
  - Make sure to complete the same chart as you did in video one and two.
  - Write a summary of your videotape, both verbal and nonverbal behavior.
  - Write a 2–3 page analysis based on your focus.
  - Make sure to describe your strengths and what you will do differently next time.
  - Discuss how you positioned yourself, your students, and how students positioned you.
  - How might these positionings be shaped by how you were taught? By the kind of school you attended? By your race, class, gender, and/or sexuality?
  - How did these positionings align (or not) with your desired teacher identities?
  - In a final paragraph state what you have learned from doing video analysis. Does it help to think about how to position yourself and your students? How students position you?

Table A.1

Evidence from video	How did you position yourself as a teacher?	How did you position your students as readers, writers, and/or participants?	How did students position you as a teacher?
Example one:			
Example two:			
Example three:			

Bibliography

Adler, S.M. (2011). Teacher epistemology and collective narratives: Interrogating teaching and diversity. *Teaching and Teacher Education: An International Journal of Research and Studies, 27*(3), 609–618.
Agee, J. (2004). Negotiating a teacher identity: An African American teacher's struggle to teach in test driven contexts. *Teachers College Record, 106*(4), 747–774.
Alexander, R. (2008). *Essays on pedagogy.* London, UK: Routledge.
Allwright, R.L. (1980). Turns, topics, and tasks: Patterns of participation in language learning and teaching. In D. Larsen-Freeman (Ed.), *Discourse analysis in second language research* (pp 165–187). Rowley, MA: Newbury House.
Alsup, J. (2006). *Teacher identity discourses: Negotiating personal and professional spaces.* Mahwah, NJ: Lawrence Erlbaum.
Anzaldua, G. (1999). *Borderlands-La Frontera: The New Mestiza.* San Francisco, CA: Aunt Lute Books.
Applebee, A., Langer, J., Nystrand, M., & Gamoran, A. (2003). Discussion based approaches to developing understanding: Classroom instruction and student performance in middle and high school English. *American Educational Research Journal, 40*(3), 685–730.
Assaf, L. (2005). Exploring identities in a reading specialization program. *Journal of Literacy Research, 37*(2), 201–236.
Baecher, L., & Kung, S.C. (2011). Jumpstarting novice teachers' ability to analyze classroom video: Affordances of an online workshop. *Journal of Digital Learning in Teacher Education, 28*(1), 16–26.
Balfanz, R., & Byrnes, V. (2012). *The importance of being there: A report on absenteeism in the nation's public schools.* Baltimore, MD: Johns Hopkins Univesity School of Education, Everyone Graduates Center, Get Schooled, 1–46.
Balfanz, R., & Legters, N. (2004). *Locating the dropout crisis. Which high schools produce the nation's dropouts? Where are they located? Who attends them?* Report 70. Johns Hopkins University: Center for Research on the Education of Students Placed at Risk CRESPAR.
Barnes, D.R., Britton, J.N., & Torbe, M. (1986). *Language, the learner and the school.* Westminster, UK: Penguin.
Beijaard, D., Meijer, P.C., & Verloop, N. (2004). Reconsidering research on teachers' professional identity. *Teaching and teacher education, 20*(2), 107–128.
Bettez, S. (2011). Critical community building: Beyond belonging. *Educational Foundations, 25,* 3–19.
Boling, E.C. (2007). Linking technology, learning, and stories: Implications from research on hypermedia video-cases. *Teaching and Teacher Education, 23,* 189–200.
Blomberg, G., Renkl, A., Sherin, M. G., Borko, H., & Seidel, T. (2013). Five research-based heuristics for using video in preservice teacher education. *Journal for Educational Research Online, 5*(1), 3–33.

Bolgatz, J. (2005). *Talking race in the classroom*. New York, NY: Teachers College Press

Borko, H., Jacobs, J., Eiteljorg, E., & Pittman, M. E. (2008). Video as a tool for fostering productive discussions in mathematics professional development. *Teaching and Teacher Education, 24*, 417–436.

Borko, H., Koellner, K., Jacobs, J., & Seago, N. (2011). Using video representations of teaching in practice-based professional development programs. *ZDM, 43*(1), 175–187.

Bourdieu, P. (1991). *Language and symbolic power*. Cambridge, MA: Harvard University Press.

Britzman, D. P. (1994). Is there a problem with knowing thyself? Toward a poststructuralist view of teacher identity. In T. Shanahan (Ed.), *Teachers thinking, teachers knowing: Reflections on literacy and language education* (pp. 53–75). Urbana, IL: National Council of Teachers of English.

Brooke, R. (1987). Underlife and writing instruction. *College Composition and Communication, 38*, 141–152.

Brophy, J. (2004). Discussion. In J. Brophy (Ed.), *Using video in teacher education: Advances in research on teaching* (Vol. 10, pp. 287–304). Amsterdam: Elsevier.

Butler, J. (1993). *Bodies that matter: on the discourse limits of "sex."* New York: Routledge.

Buzzelli, C., & Johnston, B. (2001). Authority, power, and morality in classroom discourse. *Teaching and Teacher Education, 17*, 873–884.

Carlson, H. L., & Falk, D. R., (1990). Effectiveness of interactive videodisc instructional programs in elementary teacher education. *Journal of Educational Technology Systems, 19*(2), 151–163.

Cazden, C. (2001). *Classroom discourse: The language of teaching and learning*. Portsmouth, NH: Heinemann.

Chavez-Reyes, C. (2012). Engaging in critical social dialogue with socially diverse undergraduate teacher candidates at a California State University. *Teacher Education Quarterly, 39*(2), 43–62.

Christensen, L. (2000). *Reading, writing, and rising up: Teaching about social justice and the power of the written word*. Milwaukee, WI: Rethinking Schools.

Clarke, L. (2006). Power through voicing others: Girls' positioning of boys in literature circle discussions. *Journal of Literacy Research, 38*(1), 53–79.

Cochran-Smith, M. (2004). *Walking the road: Race, diversity, and social justice in teacher education*. New York, NY: Teachers College Press.

Cochran-Smith, M., & Lytle, S. L. (2009). *Inquiry as stance: Practitioner research for the next generation*. New York, NY: Teachers College Press.

Coldron, J., & Smith, R. (1999). Active location in teachers' construction of their professional identities. *Journal of curriculum studies, 31*(6), 711–726.

Cooper, K., & Olson, M. R. (1996). Chapter 7: The Multiple "I's" of Teacher Identity. In R. T. Boak, W. R. Bond, D. Dworet, & M. Kompf (Eds.), *Changing research and practice: Teachers' professionalism, identities, and knowledge* (p. 78). London, UK: Routledge Falmer.

Corbin, J., & Strauss, A. (2007). *Basics of qualitative research: Techniques and procedures for developing grounded theory* (3rd ed.). Thousand Oaks, CA: Sage.

Cruz-Janzen, M. I. (2000). From our readers: Preparing preservice teacher candidates for leadership in equity. *Equity & Excellence in Education, 33*(1), 94–101.

Cummins, J. (2009): Pedagogies of choice: Challenging coercive relations of power in classrooms and communities. *International Journal of Bilingual Education and Bilingualism, 12*(3), 261–271.

Daniel, B. (2009). Conversations on race in teacher education cohorts. *Teaching Education, 20*(2), 175–188.

Danielewicz, J. (2001). *Teaching selves: Identity, pedagogy, and teacher education.* Albany, NY: State University of New York Press.

Darling-Hammond, L. (2010). Teacher education and the American future. *Journal of Teacher Education, 61*(1–2), 35–47.

Davies, B., & Harré, R. (1990). Positionings: The discursive production of selves. In B. Davies (Ed.), *A body of writing* (pp. 87–106). New York, NY: AltaMira Press.

Day, C. (Ed.). (1999). *Developing teachers: The challenges of lifelong learning.* Philadelphia, PA: Psychology Press.

Benton DeCorse, C. J., & Vogtle, S. P. (1997). In a complex voice: The contradictions of male elementary teachers' career choice and professional identity. *Journal of Teacher Education, 48*(1), 37.

De Freitas, M. (2006). Performing curriculum: Building ethos through narratives in pedagogical discourse. *Teachers College Record, 108*(4), 489–528.

DePalma, R. (2010). Toward a practice of polyphonic dialogue in multicultural teacher education. *Curriculum Inquiry, 40*(3), 436–453.

Dyson, A. H. (1993). *Social worlds of children: Learning to write in an urban primary school.* New York: Teachers College Press.

Elizabeth, T., Anderson, T., Snow, E., & Selman, R. (2012). Academic discussions: An analysis of instructional discourse and an argument for an integrative assessment framework. *American Educational Research Journal, 49*(6), 1214–1250.

Erikson, E. H. (1968). *Identity: Youth and crisis* (No. 7). New York: WW Norton & Company.

Fairbanks, C. M., Duffy, G. G., Faircloth, B., He, Y., Levin, B., Rohr, J., & Stein, C. (2010). Beyond knowledge: Exploring why some teachers are more thoughtfully adaptive than others. *Journal of Teacher Education, 61*, 161–171.

Fecho, B., Collier, N. D., Friese, E. E. G., & Wilson, A. (2010). Critical conversations: Tensions and opportunities of the dialogical classroom. *English Education, 42*(4), 427–447.

Florio-Ruane, S. (2002). More light: An argument for complexity in studies of teaching and teacher education. *Journal of Teacher Education, 53*(3), 205–215.

Foucault, M. (1979). *Discipline and punish: The birth of the prison.* New York, NY: Vintage.

Freedman, S. W., & Appleman, D. (2008). "What else would I be doing?": Teacher identity and teacher retention in urban schools. *Teacher Education Quarterly, 35*(3), 109–126.

Frederick, R., Cave, A., & Perencevich, K. C. (2010). Teacher candidates' transformative thinking on issues of social justice. *Teaching and Teacher Education: An International Journal of Research and Studies, 26*(2), 315–322.

Freire, P. (2000). *Pedagogy of the oppressed* (30th ed.). New York, NY: Continuum International Publishing Group.

Gay, G. (2010). *Culturally responsive teaching.* New York, NY: Teachers College Press.

Gee, J. P. (2000). Identity as an analytic lens for research in education. *Review of Research in Education, 25*, 99–125.

Gee, J. P. (2005). *An introduction to discourse analysis theory and method* (2nd ed.). New York: Routledge.

Gee, J. P. (2011). *Tools for discourse analysis.* London, UK: Routledge.

Giroux, H. (2000). *Stealing innocence: Corporate culture's war on children.* New York, NY: Palgrave.

González, N., Moll, L. C., & Amanti, C. (Eds.). (2013). *Funds of knowledge: Theorizing practices in households, communities, and classrooms.* New York, NY: Routledge.

Grossman, P., Compton, C., Igra, D., Ronfeldt, M., Shahan, E., & Williamson, P. W. (2009). Teaching practice: A cross-professional perspective. *Teachers College Record, 111*(9), 2055–2100.

Guinier, L. 2004. From racial liberalism to racial literacy: Brown v. Board and the interest divergence dilemma. *The Journal of American History, 91*(1), 92–118.

Gutierrez, K., Rymes, B., & Larson, J. (1995). Script, counterscript and underlife in the classroom: James Brown versus Brown v. The Board of Education. *Harvard Educational Review, 65*(3), 445–471.

Handsfield, L. J., Crumpler, T. P., & Dean, T. R. (2010). Tactical negotiations and creative adaptations: The discursive production of literacy curriculum and teacher identities across space-times. *Reading Research Quarterly, 45*(4), 405–431.

Haniford, L. (2010). Tracing one teacher candidate's discursive identity work. *Teaching and Teacher Education, 26*, 987–996.

Heath, S. B. (1983). *Ways with words: Language, life and work in communities and classrooms*. Cambridge, MA: Cambridge University Press.

Holland, D., Skinner, D., Lachicotte, W., & Cain, C. (1998). *Identity and agency in cultural worlds*. Cambridge, MA: Harvard University Press.

Horn, I. S., Nolen, S. B., Ward, C., & Campbell, S. S. (2008). Developing practices in multiple worlds: The role of identity in learning to teach. *Teacher Education Quarterly, 35*, 61–72.

Jackson, A. Y. (2001). Multiple Annies: Feminist poststructural theory and the making of a teacher. *Journal of Teacher Education, 52*(5), 386–397.

Janks, H. (2010). *Literacy and power*. New York: NY: Routledge.

Juzwik, M. M., Borsheim-Black, C., Caughlan, S., & Heintz, S. (2013). *Inspiring dialogue: Talking to learn in the English classroom*. New York, NY: Teacher College Press.

Juzwik, M. M., & Ives, D. (2010). Small stories as resources for performing teacher identity. *Narrative Inquiry, 20*(1), 37–61.

Juzwik, M. M., Nystrand, M., Kelly, S., & Sherry, M. (2008). Oral narrative genres as dialogic resources for classroom literature study: A contextualized case study. *American Educational Research Journal, 45*, 1111–1154.

Kea, C. D., Trent, S. C., & Davis, C. P. (2002). African American student teachers' perceptions about preparedness to teach students from culturally and linguistically diverse backgrounds. *Multicultural Perspectives, 4*(1), 18–25.

Kellner, D. (2000). Multiple literacies and critical pedagogies. In P. P. Trifonas (Ed.), *Revolutionary pedagogies—Cultural politics, instituting education, and the discourse of theory* (pp. 362–408). New York, NY: Routledge.

Kerby, A. P. (1991). *Narrative and the self*. Bloomington, IN: Indiana University Press.

Kleinknecht, M., & Schneider, J. (2013). What do teachers think and feel when analyzing videos of themselves and other teachers teaching? *Teaching and Teacher Education, 33*, 13–23.

Koc, Y., Peker, D., & Osmoanoglu, A. (2009). Supporting teacher professional development through online video case study discussions: An assemblage of preservice and inservice teachers and the case teacher. *Teaching and Teacher Education, 8*, 1158–1168.

Krammer, K., Ratzka, N., Klieme, E., Lipowsky, F., Pauli, C., & Reusser, K. (2006). Learning with classroom videos: Conception and first results of an online teacher-training program. *Zeitschrift für Didaktik der Mathematik, 38*(5), 422–432.

Labbo, L. D., Kinzer, C. K., Leu, D., & Teal, W. H. (2004). Technology: Connections that enhance children's literacy acquisition and reading achievement. In *Case Technologies to Enhance Literacy Learning*. Retrieved October 26, 2013, from http://ctell.uconn.edu/cases.htm

Ladson-Billings, G. (1991). Beyond multicultural illiteracy. *Journal of Negro Education*, 60(2), 147–57.
Lampert, M., & Ball, D.L. (1998). *Teaching, multimedia, and mathematics: Investigations of real practice*. New York, NY: Teachers College Press.
Larson, J., & Irvine, P. (1999). "We call him Dr. King": Reciprocal distancing in urban classrooms. *Language Arts*, 65(5), 393–400.
Lave, J., & Wenger, E. (1991). *Situated learning: Legitimate peripheral participation*. Cambridge, UK: Cambridge University Press.
Lazar, A.M., Edwards, P.A., & McMillon, G.T. (2012). *Bridging literacy and equity: The essential guide to social equity teaching*. New York, NY: Teachers College Press.
Leander, K. (2002). Locating Latayna: The situated production of identity artifacts in classroom interactions. *Research in the Teaching of English*, 37, 198–250.
Le Fevre, D.M. (2004). Designing for teacher learning: Video-based curriculum design. In J. Brophy (Ed.), *Using video in teacher education* (pp. 235–258). Amsterdam, Netherlands: Elsevier.
Leland, C., Harste, J., Ociepka, A., Lewison, M. & Vasquez, V. (1999). Exploring critical literacy: You can hear a pin drop. *Language Arts*, 77(1), 70–77.
Levine-Rasky, C. (2000). Framing whiteness: Working through the tensions in introducing whiteness to educators. *Race, Ethnicity and Education*, 3(3), 271–292.
Lewison, M., Flint, A.S., & Van Sluys, K. (2002). Taking on critical literacy: The journey of newcomers and novices. *Language Arts*, 79(5), 382–392.
Linehan, C., & McCarthy, J. (2000). Positioning in practice: Understanding participation in the social world. *Journal for the Theory of Social Behaviour*, 30, 435–453.
Ma, J.Y., & Singer-Gibella, M. (2011). Learning to teach in the figured world of reform mathematics: Negotiating new models of identity. *Journal of Teacher Education*, 62(1), 8–22.
MacPherson, S. (2010). Teachers' collaborative conversations about culture: Negotiating decision making in intercultural teaching. *Journal of Teacher Education*, 61(3), 271–286.
Marshall, J.D., Smagorinsky, P., & Smith, M.W. (1995). *The language of interpretation: Patterns of discourse in discussions of literature*. NCTE Research Report No. 27. Urbana, IL: National Council of Teachers of English.
McIntyre, A. (1997). *Making meaning of Whiteness: Exploring racial identity with White teachers*. Albany, NY: State University of New York Press.
McLaren, P. (1998). *Life in schools. An introduction to critical pedagogy in the foundations of education*. New York, NY: Pearson.
Mead, G.H., & Mind, H. (1934). *Self and society*. Chicago: University of Chicago Press.
Mehan, H. (1979). *Learning lessons: Social organization in the classroom*. Cambridge, MA: Harvard University Press.
Mercer, N. (2000). *Words and minds: How we use language together*. London: Routledge.
Milner, H.R. (2006). Preservice teachers' learning about cultural and racial diversity: Implications for Urban Education. *Urban Education*, 41(4), 343–375.
Mishler, E.G. (2004). Historians of the self: Restorying lives, revising identities. *Research in Human Development*, 1(1–2), 101–121.
Moje, E., & Lewis, C. (2007). Examining opportunities to learn literacy: The role of critical sociocultural literacy research. In C. Lewis, P. Enciso, & E. Moje (Eds.), *Reframing sociocultural research on literacy* (pp. 15–48). New York, NY: Lawrence Erlbaum Associates.
Mosley, M. (2010). Becoming a literacy teacher: Approximations in critical literacy teaching. *Teaching Education*, 21(4), 403–426.

Murphy, P. K., Wilkinson, I. A. G., Soter, A. O., Hennessey, M. N., & Alexander, J. F. (2009). Examining the effects of classroom discussion on students' high-level comprehension of text: A meta-analysis. *Journal of Educational Psychology, 101*(3), 740–764.

Nystrand, M., & Gamoran, A. (1991). Instructional discourse, student engagement, and literature achievement. *Research in the Teaching of English, 25*(3), 261–290.

Nystrand, M., Gamoran, N., Kachur, R., & Prendergast, C. (1997). *Opening dialogue: Understanding the dynamics of language and learning in the English classroom*. New York, NY: Teachers College Press.

Orland-Barak, L., & Yinon, H. (2007). When theory meets practice: What student teachers learn from guided reflection on their own classroom discourse. *Teaching and Teacher Education, 23*(6), 957–969.

Overbaugh, R. C. (1995) The efficacy of interactive video for teaching basic classroom management skills to pre-service teachers. *Computers in Human Behavior, 11*(3–4), 511–527.

Parker, B., & Howard, A. (2009). Beyond economics: Using social class life-based literary narratives with pre-service and practicing social studies and English teachers. *High School Journal, 92*(3), 3–13.

Pennington, J. L. (2007). Silence in the classroom/whispers in the halls: Autoethnography as pedagogy in White pre-service teacher education. *Race Ethnicity and Education, 10*(1), 93–113.

Pewewardy, C. (2005). Shared journaling: A methodology for engaging White preservice students into multicultural education discourse. *Teacher Education Quarterly, 32*(1), 41–60.

Puvirajah, A., Verma, G., & Webb, H. (2012). Examining the mediation of power in a collaborative community: Engaging in informal science as authentic practice. *Cultural Studies of Science Education, 7*, 375–408.

Reeves, J. (2009). Teacher investment in learner identity. *Teaching and Teacher Education, 25*(1), 34–41.

Rex, L. A., & Green, J. L. (2007). Classroom discourse and interaction: Reading across the traditions. In B. Spolsky & F. M. Hult (Eds.), *International handbook of educational linguistics* (pp. 571–584). London: Blackwell.

Rex, L. A., & Schiller, L. (2009). *Using discourse analysis to improve classroom interaction*. New York, NY: Routledge.

Rich, P. (2015). Examining the role of others in video self analysis. In B. Calandra & P. J. Rich (Eds.), *Digital video for teacher education: Research and practice* (pp. 71–88). New York, NY: Routledge.

Ritchie, S., Rigano, D., & Lowry, J. (2000). Shifting power relations in the "getting of wisdom." *Teaching and Teacher Education, 16*, 165–177.

Rogers, R., & Christian, J. (2007). 'What could I say?': A critical discourse analysis of the construction of race in children's literature. *Race Ethnicity and Education, 10*(1), 21–46.

Rogers, T., Marshall, E., & Tyson, C. A. (2006). Dialogic narratives of literacy, teaching, and schooling: Preparing literacy teachers for diverse settings. *Reading Research Quarterly, 41*(2), 202–224. doi:10.1598/RRQ.41.2.3

Ronfeldt, M., & Grossman, P. (2008). Becoming a professional: Experimenting with possible selves in professional preparation. *Teacher Education Quarterly, 35*, 41–60.

Rosaen, C., Lundeberg, M., Cooper, M., Fritzen, A., & Terpstra, M. (2008). Noticing noticing: How does investigation of video records change how teachers reflect on their experiences? *Journal of Teacher Education, 59*(4), 347–360.

Roth, W. M. (2007). Epistemic mediation: Video data as filters for the objectification of teaching by teachers. In R. Goldman, R. Pea, B. Barron, & S. J. Derry (Eds.), *Video research in the learning sciences* (pp. 367–382). Mahwah, NJ: Lawrence Erlbaum.

Santagata, R., & Guarino, J. (2011). Using video to teach future teachers to learn from teaching. *ZDM the International Journal of Mathematics Education, 43*(1), 133–145.

Schieble, M. (2012a). A critical discourse analysis of teachers' views on LGBT literature. *Discourse: Studies in the Cultural Politics of Education, 33*(2), 207–222.

Schieble, M. (2012b). Critical conversations on Whiteness with young adult literature. *Journal of Adolescent and Adult Literacy, 56*(3), 212–221.

Sexton, D. M. (2008). Student teachers negotiating identity, role and agency. *Teacher Education Quarterly, Summer*, 73–88.

Sfard, A., & Prusak, A. (2005). Telling identities: In search of an analytic tool for investigating learning as a culturally shaped activity. *Educational Researcher, 34*(4), 14–22.

Sherin, M. G. (2004). New perspectives on the role of video in teacher education. In J. Brophy (Ed.), *Using video in teacher education* (pp. 1–27). New York: Elsevier Science.

Sherin, M. G., & Han, S. (2004). Teacher learning in the context of a video club. *Teaching and Teacher Education, 20*, 163–183.

Sherin, M. G., & Russ, R. S. (2015). Teacher noticing via video: The role of interpretive frames. In B. Calandra & P. J. Rich (Eds.), *Digital video for teacher education: Research and practice* (pp. 3–20). New York: Routledge.

Sherin, M. G., & van Es, E. (2009). Effects of video club participation on teacher's professional vision. *Journal of Teacher Education, 60*(1), 20–37.

Skerrett, A. (2011). English teachers' racial literacy knowledge and practice. *Race Ethnicity and Education, 14*(3), 313–330.

Sleeter, C. E. (2008). Critical family history, identity, and historical memory. *Educational Studies: Journal of the American Educational Studies Association, 43*(2), 114–124.

Sleeter, C. E. (2011). Becoming White: Reinterpreting a family story by putting race back into the picture. *Race, Ethnicity and Education, 14*(4), 421–433.

Sleeter, C., Torres, M. N., & Laughlin, P. (2004). Scaffolding conscientization through inquiry in teacher education. *Teacher Education Quarterly, 31*(1), 81–96.

Smagorinsky, P., Cook, L. S., Moore, C., Jackson, A. Y., & Fry, P. G. (2004). Tensions in learning to teach: Accommodation and the development of a teaching identity. *Journal of Teacher Education, 55*(1), 8–24.

Smith, K. (2001). Critical conversations in difficult times. *English Education, 33*(2), 153–165.

Spiro, R. J., Collins, B. P., & Ramchandran, A. (2007). Reflections on a post-Gutenberg epistemology of video use in ill-structured domains: Fostering complex learning and cognitive flexibility. In R. Goldman, R. Pea, B. Barron, & S. J. Derry (Eds.), *Video research in the learning sciences* (pp. 93–100). Mahwah, NJ: Lawrence Erlbaum.

Sugrue, C. (1997). Student teachers' lay theories and teaching identities: Their implications for professional development. *European Journal of Teacher Education, 20*(3), 213–225.

Tripp, T., & Rich, P. (2012). Using video to analyze one's own teaching. *British Journal of Educational Technology, 43*(4), 678–704.

Twine, F. W. (2004). A White side of Black Britain: The concept of racial literacy. *Ethnic and racial studies, 27*(6), 878–907.

van Es, E. (2009). Participants' roles in the context of a video club. *Journal of the Learning Sciences, 18*(1), 100–137.

van Es, E., & Sherin, M. G. (2002). Learning to notice: Scaffolding new teachers interpretations of classroom interactions. *Journal of Technology and Teacher Education, 10*(4), 571–596.

Vaught, S. E., & Castagno, A. E. (2008). "I don't think I'm a racist": Critical race theory, teacher attitudes, and structural racism. *Race Ethnicity and Education, 11*(2), 95–113.

Vetter, A. (2010). Positioning students as readers and writers: An examination of teacher's improvised responses in a high school English classroom. *English Education, 43*(1), 33–64.

Vetter, A., Meacham, M., & Schieble, M. (2013). Leveling the field: Negotiating positions of power as a preservice teacher. *Action in Teacher Education, 35*(4), 230–251.

Vetter, A., Myers, J., & Hester, M. (2014). Negotiating ideologies about teaching writing in a high school English classroom. *The Teacher Educator, 49*(1), 10–27.

Villegas, A. M., & Irvine, J. J. (2010). Diversifying the teaching force: An examination of major arguments. *The Urban Review, 42*(3), 175–192.

Vygotsky, L. S. (1978). Mind and society: The development of higher mental processes.

Watson, C. (2006). Narratives of practice and the construction of identity in teaching. *Teachers and Teaching: Theory and Practice, 12*(5), 509–526.

Wortham, S. (2004). From good student to outcast: The emergence of a classroom identity. *Ethos, 32*(2), 164–187.

Zeichner, K. M., & National Center for Research on Teacher Learning. (1993). *Educating teachers for cultural diversity*. NCRTL Special Report. Retrieved November 21, 2014, from http://ncrtl.msu.edu/http/sreports/sr293.pdf

Index

advocacy 54–73: analysis charts for positions of advocacy 68; chart for discourse analysis of power positions 68; enacting an advocate identity 59–63; moments of struggle 63–65; positions of 54–73; teaching students 70
Alsup, J. 11–16

Blomberg, G. 5

checklist for video recording in K–12 Schools 123
critical conversations 99–100; 125; characteristics of critical conversations 99; colorblind discourses 105; gender and sexual orientation 101–104; in teacher education 95–97; model critical conversation 99; preservice teachers critical conversations 98–99; race, class, and gender 104–108
critical literacy 97–98
culturally relevant pedagogy 34, 56, 67
culturally responsive teaching 14, 55–56, 125

Davies, B. 18–19
decomposing practice 3–5
dialogically organized instruction 20; 76; addressivity 76; analysis guide for dialogic teaching 89; dialogic instruction 75–78; monologic 76–77
discourse analysis 17, 19–21, 21–23, 115, 119–120; classroom discourse 20–23; discourse analysis chart for video-recorded lesson 22; discourse communities 19
discourse participation patterns 83–84; micro-level 65; macro-level 66; resources for practice 120
discourse patterns 24–28; initiation-respond-evaluate patterns 71, 75; posing questions 78–83; 84–8; responding to students 78–83, 84–87

Facilitative Teaching 74–103; analysis chart for positions of facilitative teaching 89; positions of 74–103

Gee, J. 12–13, 21
Grossman, P. 3, 16
Guinier, L. 98

Harre, R. 18–19
Holland, D. 12–14

identity 12–14; agency 16; identity markers 15, 19; identity and power 15; theories about identity 12–14
identity work 2; alignments and misalignments 114–116; implications for 114–119; in teacher education 14–18; 114–119; troubleshooting identity work in teacher education 119–125
interactionally aware 17; interactional awareness 17, 20, 77

Juzwik, M. 34–35, 61, 75–77, 83–84

Lazar, A. 55–57
Lewison, M. 97–98

Nystrand, M. 16, 75, 86, 98

Parental Permission Form 123
positioning theory 18–19; first-order positionings 18–19; interactive positionings 18–19, 23, 116–118; reflexive positionings 18–19, 23; second-order positionings 19; third-order positionings 19
power 32–53; analysis chart for positions of power 48; chart for discourse analysis of power positions 48; negotiating power in the classroom 34; positions of 32–53; power-share identity 35–36; power-control identity 40–45

racial literacy 97–98
Rex, L. 16–18, 20, 45, 114

Sherin, M. G. 4, 45–46, 55
Skerrett, A. 98
social equity teaching 55–57
study context 6–8

teacher identities 14; advocate 57–59; alignments and misalignments 114–115; authoritative 34–35; critical pedagogy 32. 36; facilitator 24–28; framework for exploring teacher identities through video 17; identity kit 13

Van Es, E. 4, 45–46, 55
Video-Based Response and Revision 20
video analysis: additional resources 124; assignment 22, 127; of teaching 3–5; teacher preparation 2–3

For Product Safety Concerns and Information please contact our EU
representative GPSR@taylorandfrancis.com
Taylor & Francis Verlag GmbH, Kaufingerstraße 24, 80331 München, Germany

www.ingramcontent.com/pod-product-compliance
Lightning Source LLC
Chambersburg PA
CBHW061843300426
44115CB00013B/2492